ANXIETY THERAPY WORKBOOK

A HOLISTIC & SPIRITUAL APPROACH

i

First published in 2022 by Amazon.
© Paul Craddock. Version 1.1 22nd November 2022

Designed by Paul Craddock, printed and bound in the UK by Amazon

Disclaimer

This workbook is intended to complement and support, not replace normal allopathic medicine or medical treatment. If you suffer from any acute or chronic disease you should always seek medical attention from a qualified doctor immediately. The author and publisher accept no liability or damage of any nature resulting directly or indirectly from the application or use of any information contained within this workbook.

The author and publisher of this workbook and the accompanying materials have used their best efforts in preparing this book. The author and publisher make no representation or warranties with respect to the accuracy, applicability, fitness or completeness of the contents of this workbook. The information contained in this workbook is strictly for educational purposes. Therefore, if you wish to apply ideas and techniques contained in this workbook, you are taking full responsibility for your actions.

ACKNOWLEDGEMENTS

Rachel Craddock for the clouds front cover & the author's photograph

Proofread by Trish Mills

Tim Chaloner for the heart drawing

SECTIONS & EXERCISES

1. Preface & Introduction

I experienced a difficult and traumatic childhood and was left to deal with the resulting anxiety, stress, and psychological problems in adulthood. And so, in my late teenage years in the 1980s I embarked on a journey of research and self-discovery to try to help myself. Mainstream health care was no help, but, fortunately, I found the alternative methods and therapies that worked for me. So, after recovering, I eventually trained in psychotherapy and hypnotherapy and at one time was running a successful practice from three separate clinics in different towns.

I found that the type of therapy I had experienced personally also helped many other people. Just after I started my therapy practice, a lady phoned me saying she was about to jump out of a high window. I managed to persuade her to come for an immediate consultation. After a series of consultations, she made a complete recovery and went on to recommend countless people to me. This was much appreciated as I built my practice!

Having helped many people over the years, I have discovered that the therapy can take a number of sessions. I found that on average it takes about eight hour long weekly sessions but, in some cases, it needs 20 or more. Some of the more severe cases would need considerably more sessions than that. This meant there were potentially issues of the patient being unable to afford the ongoing cost of the weekly sessions, being unable to travel from a distance and not persevering with their therapy to enable a successful outcome.

The aim of this course is, therefore, to make the necessary therapy to help with anxiety, emotional problems, psychological problems and stress affordable and available to everybody. One to one sessions with a therapist are desirable. However, even if you were seeing a therapist, I would expect that you would still be working through the techniques, and therapies in this course which I have written specifically as a self-help guide. I have successfully used the methods outlined in this course extensively myself and with patients. And therefore, I can vouch for their effectiveness.

Please now go to the next section on "How to use this course".

2. How to Use This Course

"It isn't what you have, or who you are, or where you are, or what you are doing that makes you unhappy. It is what you think about". Dale Carnegie

The program in this course is designed to progressively reduce the effects of anxiety, stress and the symptoms of the complete range of emotional and psychological problems from which humanity suffers from today. If you stick with me and persevere, I would expect you to be able to completely recover from your symptoms. However, even if you are absolutely fine with no stress, anxiety or mental health problems whatsoever, if practiced regularly, you should gain immense benefit from the meditation techniques.

While not used by most mainstream mental health centres and hospitals who tend to favour prescription drug-based therapy, the methods and knowledge in this course has been widely tried and tested throughout the world over many years. Maybe you have tried taking prescription drugs and are now ready to take an alternative more natural approach? If you are currently taking prescription drugs, work through this course but consult your doctor before coming off them.

I strongly recommend that you work through this course in the order that I suggest. That said, you can refer to the fast help section at any time to get immediate help to reduce a negative symptom currently being experienced. The Fast Help section is for immediate temporary help and the other sections then worked through in the correct order, are designed to progressively reduce, and then permanently remove anxiety, stress and negative symptoms.

The next section, which is the Initial Consultation, is adapted from my on-site face to face initial consultations I have given over many years. This gives you an explanation and understanding of why you may be experiencing the type of problems you are currently suffering from and the way forward.

At the end of the initial consultation, I will introduce you to your Course Journal. This is an essential support tool for you to use as you work through this course, and it will become like a good friend! Additionally, if you subscribe to the premium version of this course, your tutor can review your journal ongoing as you progress and give you support. Journaling is a very effective therapy on its own. I will cover journaling in detail. The section after the journal section is the Fast Help Section where you will be able to get immediate help.

After the Fast Help Section, you will work through the Introduction to Meditation Section, the Meditation Practice Section and the Thought & Emotion Control Section in that order. You will then have some amazing tools to remove anxiety, reduce mental health problems, negative thoughts and stress. When you finish the Thought & Emotion Control Section, the Spiritual Part Section deserves a visit, it will provide some empowering essential spiritual knowledge whether you are ready for it or not! This type of knowledge forms part of many powerful organisations teachings such as the Transcendental Meditation (TM) organisation. Many leaders and well-known celebrities are associated with the Transcendental Meditation Organisation.

The hypnotherapy section explains all about hypnosis, hypnotherapy and self-hypnosis. This is in preparation for the following Memory & Emotion Recall Section. If you have been working progressively through the exercises, the self-hypnosis audio guide will effortlessly complement what you have already learnt and are familiar with.

Last but certainly not least, the Memory & Emotion Recall section. In this section you will be using a tried and tested technique to permanently remove the type of symptoms covered in the Initial Consultation Section. While working through the Memory & Emotion Recall Section, you should still be practicing in your meditation sessions. Daily meditation practice is a beneficial continuous lifestyle choice. Continue using the Fast Help Section throughout this course whenever you feel the need.

The Memory & Emotion Recall Section utilises a weekly session along with journal work. Use it until you are happy your symptoms have gone or considerably reduced. I will warn you, however, you will need to persist, if you do you will arrive at your ideal destination.

So, there you have it, you have some powerful self-help techniques available, but you must decide right now to work through them continuously. You must persevere, you really must! I cannot emphasise that enough! The alternative is that you are possibly, not going to resolve and completely release the underlying cause of your symptoms in order to feel much better! So, visualise the outcome you want for yourself and make a commitment to yourself to work towards it. After all, you will only be letting yourself down if you don't.

Ask yourself where you want to be in a year from now? Feeling much better and free from your problem, I guess? So, I want you to imagine two different scenarios: the first one is that you have not persistently and consistently worked through this course and have experienced no significant improvement. Now imagine how you will feel about yourself in one years' time if this is the case? Take a few moments to really think about that scenario. Now come back to the present and then go a year ahead in your imagination again. And the situation this time, is that you have persevered and worked through this course and are feeling considerably better.

Having considered how you will feel in a years' time when either you have or have not, persevered and worked through this course. Which path are you going to take? I thought so, I will see you at the Initial Consultation Section!

3 Your Initial Consultation

"Most men occasionally stumble over the truth but most pick themselves up and continue as if nothing had happened". Winston Churchill

This section is in the form of an initial consultation which I have undertaken countless times face to face with clients in my consulting rooms. During this initial consultation, I usually obtain information about the "problem", explain how this "problem" may have arisen and the steps, techniques and methods we need to follow to help them overcome it.

Whilst we may have a slight disadvantage here because you're not sitting in front of me because you have enrolled on this Workbook course, I already know something significant about you! This is because most people who consult me are either doing something they don't want to do or, are not doing something they do want to do. Another way of putting it would be to say that you are suffering from something inside of yourself but outside of your control. You could also say that you are experiencing a feeling or emotion that you would rather not have, and you have no control over it.

So, you are likely to be suffering from something inside of yourself but outside of your control. This definition covers a multitude of psychological and emotional disorders. Typically, this includes, anxiety, panic attacks, phobias, depression and mood disorders, neurotic and psychotic behaviour and compulsive out of control behaviour. If you have a psychotic disorder, you are unlikely to be reading this book. This is because a person suffering from a psychosis clearly has something wrong with them. However, they cannot understand this and think that in fact there is nothing wrong with them. With a neurosis you are aware that you have a problem and are seeking help. I should add that a psychosis is an extreme form of a neurosis. So, I would recommend seeking help whilst you are able too. Because there is a remote but nevertheless real possibility, that if you are unlucky, your neurosis could develop into a psychosis whereby you will not be in a position to seek help because you will think there is nothing wrong with you!

Some patients however, perhaps like yourself, have consulted me maybe suffering from depression, anxiety or excess stress as a result of their work, difficult personal relationships or their current stressful personal circumstances. In other words, the current situation they find themselves in is causing their symptoms rather than what has happened in the past during their childhood or from a recent single severe traumatic incident causing post-traumatic stress disorder. It is entirely possible of course, that unresolved issues from the past are adding to life's difficulties currently being experienced thus making symptoms worse.

If you can clearly identify that a current situation is causing a problem, then my explanation below under "How did I get like this?" may not entirely apply to you. But it may to a certain extent! Most of us have at least a certain number of unprocessed emotions stored from childhood. This may not be noticed and so we appear to be symptom free, until that is, it gets added to by life's current stressful event that we are now faced with. In this area of the human condition there are enough grey areas to paint a grey battleship! So, I would suggest that it may be a good idea to work through this section and take the stress test in Exercise 2, and we will take it from there!

At the end of this section, we will work through the Fast Help Section for fast relief of symptoms at any time. The other sections are there with the aim of permanently removing your symptoms, so they don't come back. My aim is to help you become the best person you could be if fate had not intervened.

How did I get like this?

The fact that there is something inside of you but outside of your control would suggest that you have previously unsuccessfully expended a vast amount of conscious mental energy trying to overcome your problem. If the problem was in your conscious mind, you would have succeeded but it is not, it's in the subconscious part of your mind not directly accessed by your conscious mind. It may be possible to get some limited help from using therapies like CBT using the conscious mind. However, as the source of the problem will be in the subconscious mind the symptoms will not completely be removed and will most likely return.

So, we have (at least) two parts to our mind. Namely, the conscious mind and the subconscious mind. Your conscious mind is the part that you think is you! This part holds your thoughts and reasoning abilities. However, you are unable to undertake more than one activity at the same time. Like reading a book and having a conversation. Your subconscious mind on the other hand, is responsible for running all your bodies processes all at the same time. For example, whilst you are reading this book, your subconscious mind is looking after all your bodily functions at the same time. Your subconscious mind controls and runs a large number of processes at the same time. It is therefore much more powerful than the conscious mind which can only really focus on one task at a time!

Accepting that if your problem was in your conscious mind, you would have rationalised and dealt with it by now, then it would be safe to assume that whatever the problem is, it resides in the subconscious part of your mind. And as your subconscious mind has control over your body, including its emotions, if something is causing it a problem, it has a vast array of symptoms to choose from to put you through. These can include physical symptoms like a nervous twitch or worse! Let us look at the symptoms which can be experienced in an anxiety attack. If you were suffering from an anxiety attack you would not necessarily experience all the symptoms listed below:

1. The heart beats alarmingly quickly
2. Increase in breathing rate as if not getting enough air (air hunger)
3. Cramped feeling across the lower part of the diaphragm
4. Tingling sensation
5. Hot or cold flush in unexpected parts of the body, usually the extremities
6. Feeling that unconsciousness may be coming
7. Rooted to the spot as if you had seen a ghost
8. Dumbstruck or immobilised
9. Panic stricken at what is happening
10. A return to normal

Examples of your subconscious mind making you behave in an out-of-control manner could also include any ceremony or ritual about daily habits that are out of the ordinary. Such as washing your hands 5 times before breakfast or turning socks inside out before putting them on. Or walking over every crack in the pavement, for example. Additionally, any silly fears such as heights, flames, knives, rats with long tails, snakes, blood, water, death, darkness, germs, cancer etc.... Also, compulsively checking things and a proneness to blushing. I could go on and will discuss later on further symptoms your subconscious mind can give you if something is disturbing it.

What causes my subconscious mind to give me these symptoms?

Your subconscious mind is there to protect you, and only you. This is because it is your subconscious mind! So, what is going on in your subconscious mind? Well, it is trying to protect you from something. Something inside of you! let me explain. Your subconscious mind has the ability to repress an emotion from the conscious mind if the conscious mind cannot deal with it. A person's subconscious mind will repress an unbearable emotion in order to protect the conscious mind.

A person's mind will repress with convenient amnesia something unbearable to that person. (i) If the incident had generated an emotion too intense for the conscious mind to process, the subconscious mind will block the memory and the emotion from conscious recall. Although sometimes the memory can remain, but the emotion has been repressed.

Another way of putting it, is that normally your conscious mind will process emotions as they arise or afterwards. However, if they are of a very intense nature the subconscious mind will repress them from conscious recall to protect your conscious mind. You then have repressed memories and emotions. Or put more simply, you have unprocessed emotions. Because your subconscious mind has kept these emotions from conscious recall, it experiences anxiety. You can experience this anxiety directly as an anxious feeling within you. Or, by the way of symptom substitution. More about this later.

An example of this would be someone who is involved in a road accident who truthfully tells the police "I remember backing my car out of the drive and remember waking up in hospital". However, I cannot remember the drive to the scene of the accident, or of the accident itself". In order to protect this person's mind from the horror of the accident, this person's subconscious mind has also repressed the memory of the rest of the journey and the journey afterwards in the ambulance.

Another example concerns an old patient of mine, this gentleman had been seeing me for around 8 sessions of hypnotherapy to get to the root cause of a problem. At one particular session he started to recall the originating incident with the accompanying intense emotion. This included intense bodily sensations, which we call an abreaction. Then all of a sudden, the recall stopped. In order to stop the abreaction, I ended the session. He then looked at me and asked who I was and where he was! Whatever he had started to bring to his conscious awareness was so traumatic and was so painful that his subconscious mine reburied it again. As it did so, he could not remember who I was or where he was. We had to call his wife to pick him up. Fortunately, over the course of the following week his recent memory slowly returned, and we were able to resume with his therapy. He had had a demonstration of the very mental prosses that had buried the original traumatic event which was causing him anxiety and an associated symptom/problem.

To help illustrate the need for the subconscious mind to repress an unresolved emotion, I will use an analogy. I want you to imagine a large tyre, this is the equivalent of your conscious mind and biological organism. Now imagine using a pump to put air into this imaginary tyre, this air is the equivalent of an intense negative emotion or trauma. The tyre can only take so much air pressure before exploding. Your conscious mind and biological organism can also only take so much intensity of emotion or trauma before metaphorically exploding into a complete breakdown. The biological organism can only take so much, and so a safety mechanism is required in that the subconscious mind hides the overload of negative emotion from conscious recall in order to prevent an overload of the mind and biological organism. However, whilst this unprocessed emotion remains blocked from conscious recall, it causes the subconscious mind anxiety.

To further illustrate, I will give you another analogy: Imagine an old-fashioned steam train. See the man on the footplate shovelling coal into the furnace to heat the boiler, now see the large locomotive boiler full of water and steam, the steam which drives the engine. The pressure keeps going up and up. If sufficient steam is not used up in driving the engine, then the pressure builds up inside the boiler. To stop the boiler blowing up under too much pressure, the steam escapes through a safety valve fitted to the top of the boiler. You too have a metaphorical safety valve to stop you metaphorically exploding, in that your subconscious mind can block the excess emotion or trauma that cannot be handled by your conscious mind.

The key here is that unprocessed feelings and emotions will produce anxiety. You can experience that anxiety directly as an anxious feeling or the anxiety can be transformed into a symptom. Subconscious anxiety within the human psyche is intolerable to the organism as a whole and will therefore produce an effect on the organism as a whole. Either mentally or physically or a combination of both, this anxiety needs to find an outlet. I am not talking about anxiety as the result of something you are consciously aware of like your job, divorce, family problems, money problems redundancy or bankruptcy, for example. I am talking about anxiety in the subconscious mind. The cause that has been hidden from the conscious mind. Therefore, no amount of thinking about it with your conscious mind will remove the anxiety. Freud talked of free-floating anxiety, nameless, formless, timeless which attaches itself to nothing. The anxiety attack I documented earlier in this section, is what Sigmund Freud had in mind when he wrote of free-floating anxiety. Meaning it was free of any known cause and just literally floated in the mind.

This free-floating anxiety is a problem to the human mind because there is nothing more disconcerting than feeling anxiety and not knowing why. Jung described anxiety as fear spread thinly. Again, there is nothing more disconcerting to the human mind than feeling fear and not knowing why.

What symptoms are possible?
Consequently, this anxiety will need to find an outlet. There are different ways this can happen. This is often determined by the personality type of the person concerned. Personality types are determined in our formative years.

Direct
You can experience anxiety directly, as a straightforward anxious feeling or you can also experience some or all of the components of an anxiety attack listed previously in this section.

Expectant anxiety

This can manifest as a general apprehensiveness, a free-floating anxiety which is ready to attach itself to any idea that is in anyway suitable. It influences judgement, selects what is to be expected, and lies in wait for any opportunity that will allow it to justify itself. This state is called expectant anxiety or anxious expectation.ii People who suffer from this kind of anxiety always have a pessimistic outlook on life and see the worst in all possibilities. Where this anxiety is not free floating, it can be bound physically and attached to particular objects or situations. This type of anxiety can manifest as a phobia as described below.

Phobias

A phobia is an irrational fear and a symbolic representation of the true subconscious anxiety. The list of phobias people can experience is extensive. Fear of open spaces closed spaces, of being sick, fear of flying, spiders, mice, blood, snakes, crowds, needles are just a few of the common ones. Any irrational fear could be considered a phobia. I am not talking about a response to real and justified danger.

Externalisation and Identification

The person's anxiety is felt inwardly and projected outwardly. People in the caring professions for example. The unknown has therefore been converted into the known. By removing the troubles of others, the person removes his or her own anxiety.

Depression

There are two common types of depression, namely reactive depression when you are depressed as the result of an external life situation, such as losing your job, the end of a relationship or just fed up with the situation you find yourself in. The other type of depression is clinical depression when you are depressed for no reason, you cannot attribute it to an outside cause. This type of depression has a subconscious cause. As does bi-polar disorder where the depression switches to a manic phase. This used to be called manic depression.

Compulsions

By obsessional actions and compulsions, I am referring to behaviours such as obsessive hand washing or following a particular ceremony, such as having to tap a door handle three times before entering or arranging objects in a certain manner, for example. I could give many more instances. The internal anxiety has been diverted and expressed in the obsessional action so the person suffering from these obsessional actions feels no anxiety. However, if the person is stopped from performing their obsessive action or attempt to give it up, they will certainly experience anxiety.

Addictive Behaviour

Addictive behaviour would be something which you are unable to control such as gambling, compulsive shopping, being an alcoholic or addicted to sex to the extent of exploiting the other person and probably many other people.

Conversion Disorder

Conversion disorder, also called functional neurological symptom disorder, and previously known as hysteria, is a disorder in which the symptoms or bodily effects cannot be explained by a neurological or a general medical condition. Psychological factors, such as subconscious anxiety and conflicts are the cause. Sigmund Freud first used the phrase conversion disorder and hypothesised that the occurrence of certain symptoms not explained by organic diseases reflect subconscious conflict.

The conversion refers to the substitution of a somatic/bodily symptom for a repressed subconscious conflict or emotion.

Examples of conversion symptoms include:

1. Blindness
2. Paralysis
3. Dystonia
4. Psychogenic nonepileptic seizures
5. Anaesthesia
6. Swallowing difficulties
7. Motor tics and bodily twitches
8. Speech symptoms such as stammering
9. Difficulty walking

Someone suffering with a conversion disorder is not feigning the signs and symptoms. Despite the lack of a definitive organic diagnosis, the patient's distress is very real and the physical symptoms they are experiencing cannot be controlled by their own will and conscious mind. So, the person is not malingering an illness.

Arguably, symptoms like migraine, skin conditions like eczema and allergies can be included under conversion disorder as the conversion refers to the substitution of a somatic/bodily symptom for a repressed subconscious conflict or emotion. Certainly, anxiety and stress can worsen these symptoms.

Hysterical Dissociation

Dissociation hysteria is also a manifestation of an underlying subconscious conflict or anxiety. But this is an escape behaviour in which the person gratifies his urges but denies the personal responsibility of his unacceptable behaviour.

Paranoia

Paranoia is a thought process influenced by subconscious anxiety and typically includes beliefs that they are being persecuted or someone is out to get them. The person can believe that they are threatened or that they are under threat by a conspiracy. Other symptoms include making false accusations and general mistrust of other people. Paranoia is generally a psychotic symptom not a neurotic symptom. So, unless you have a mild form of paranoia, as I explained earlier, you would most likely not be aware you are suffering from paranoia and so would not be reading this and if you did, you would think this does not apply to you.

Post-Traumatic Stress Disorder (PTSD)

This disorder has featured prominently in the news in recent years because of its occurrence in soldiers returning from combat. In World Wars 1 and 2 it was called shell shock. It may occur in soldiers who have witnessed a traumatic event. PTSD symptoms may include anxiety, excessive vigilance, exaggerated tendency to startle, nightmares, flashbacks to the traumatic event which may be triggered by associated memories, insomnia, outburst of anger and social withdrawal. However, Post-Traumatic Stress Disorder (PTSD) can also result from any trauma such as being raped or mugged. The intensity of the trauma was too much for the conscious mind to deal with and process and so it remains in the subconscious mind awaiting processing.

Anxiety and Sexuality

Anxiety is fear spread thinly. iii Fear causes the body to go into the fight or flight response mode directing blood mainly to the essential organs. Sexuality is therefore totally repressed. Imagine a fearful soldier about to jump out of the trenches and go into battle, again sexuality will be the last thing on his mind and totally repressed. Anxiety being fear spread thinly will not totally repress sexuality but, is still likely to inhibit it in some way. I will not elaborate any further but leave it to the readers imagination as to the possible likely inhibitions or restrictions.

Notwithstanding the above, if a person grows up with a lack of love from their parents or parent, the person can develop a low self-esteem, have low self-confidence and have a lack of love for themselves. They will therefore find it difficult to love someone else. This of course, can also be an inhibiting factor in relationships.

Lack of love for oneself and repressed emotions as I have covered earlier in this section, can result in someone being stuck in a relationship with a partner they don't love. This is because their anxiety prevents them from developing and sustaining a relationship with someone they truly do love. They will often reject someone for whom they have deep loving feelings or a great attraction for. This is a self defence mechanism in the face of anxiety.

Out of Control Thoughts

This is a problem concerned with your ego and your conscious mind. The part you think is you, the part you are thinking with right now! Your rational conscious mind is an essential and indispensable part of you. But it can also get out of control and cause you problems, huge problems! Have you ever woken up in the middle of the night and been unable to get back to sleep because you could not stop your thoughts? Or worse, you couldn't get to sleep in the first place. Do you find you cannot stop thinking about something especially if there is an emotion involved? Do you keep thinking the same thoughts and wonder what's the point I have already thought about this many times? Have you had a disagreement with someone and then keep going over the conversation in your head and then make up a conversation based on what you could have said? Do you start worrying about something and can't stop? All these are common occurrences to humans, you are not alone! The good news is that you can learn how to gain control over your thoughts. It will take some long-term practice but there are also some quick techniques I will teach you in the meantime.
Regarding the long-term practice, I will teach you techniques using meditation. Meditation is a long-term practice, but it gives you a number of benefits, including enhanced relaxation and a reduction of anxiety, which I guess you need right now!

Stress

As you work through this course you will be practicing techniques that will help to reduce stress. Most of us in the western world suffer from varying degrees of stress and walk around with a certain amount of stored stress day to day. The body is good at storing stress in its muscles, organs and fibres. An analogy of the releasing of stress in the body would be the unwinding of the twisting of the organs and fibres in the body, as the stress slowly releases.

Course Journal

To complete this section, we need to start your Course Journal. We will cover journal therapy in detail in the next section. Your Course Journal is there to support and guide you through this course. If you are subscribing to the premium version of this course, it will also enable communication and support from your tutor/therapist. Your Course Journal can be found at the end of this course or may have been supplied separately. In any case, it is always available separately as an electronic MS word file format for you to complete on your computer. This enables you to email parts of your journal to your tutor/therapist when completed, assuming you are subscribing to premium tutor support. See the resource section in the Appendix for details.

EXERCISE 1:
Go to your Course Journal and complete Exercise 1: Personal Details and Initial Consultation Form.

EXERCISE 2:
Go to your Course Journal and complete Exercise 2: The Stress Test.

After you have completed Exercise 2, the stress test, if you have subscribed to premium tutor support, wait until your first consultation with your tutor before proceeding further.

4 Your Journal

I can shake off everything as I write; my sorrows disappear, my courage is reborn."
Anne Frank

Advantages of journaling

There are considerable advantages to keeping a journal. You will discover that your journal is your friend and therapist. It will be your friend at the end of your pen. Journaling has been used as a form of effective therapy for a considerable number of years. I will guide you through how to use your journal as you progress through this course. Your Course Journal will form an essential part of this course. It runs alongside it and serves as an important communication tool with your tutor should you choose the premium course option. I will also guide you through how to set up a separate journal with different sections to run alongside your Course Journal and workbook.

Journaling records the concerns of the heart mind and soul and as you use your journal you will find it helps to get your thoughts in order. It will help you explore your feelings and beliefs and put you in touch with yourself. Your journal lets you express your thoughts and feelings and is always accessible. It is a form of self-care which helps you to get to know yourself.

Writing about your feelings helps improve your mental health. You will explore emotions and facts and see any unhelpful patterns in yourself and others. Therefore, journaling also helps you understand your relationships and importantly, helps you decide on the right conversations to have with the people with whom you have a relationship with, and thus help avoid damaging conflict. It is therefore helpful in processing intensive relationships and avoiding confrontations.

Journaling will help you to deal with traumatic events and stressful pivotal important times in your life when you have to make major decisions or find your way out of a very difficult situation in your life. You will find that you are able to work through problems and see new opportunities.

Offloading your worries on to paper stops you going over thoughts repeatedly. Have you noticed how you keep thinking the same thoughts? Writing them down cuts this crazy cycle of activity and helps you make the right decisions and helps you achieve your goals. Gaining control of your thoughts in this way helps stop negative and unproductive thoughts and so reduces stress and anxiety.

Journaling also helps improve your sleep by expressing and releasing negative thoughts and feelings and stops you going over them at night and thus keeping you awake or being unable to get back to sleep.

By regularly reviewing your journal, you can look back on your former self and see how you have evolved. You will be able to make decisions based on accurate recordings of past events and revisit memories that may be flawed in detail or lost in time. This will clarify your thinking and help track events and projects. Regularly reviewing your journal will also help with your therapy.

How to use your journal
Journaling should be private but, if you are seeing a therapist, it would be helpful to share at least some parts of it provided your therapist confirms that all communication is confidential. You will be using two journals in this course, your personal journal and the course journal. You will be able to share information from your personal journal with your tutor through your course journal should you choose that option.

Your journaling should be honest. Do not hold anything back. Completely express yourself. You may be less than honest with yourself if you are worried that someone may read your personal journal. So, take steps to keep it safe and private. This may mean using a locked drawer, filing cabinet or safe if you are using a physical paper journal. Or a password protected App or software. You can easily lock files in Microsoft Word. There are also many journaling Apps you can download on to your phone, both free and paid versions. Pictures and film can often be incorporated in electronic journals. However, for all electronic journals whether on Apps or on your computer, make sure you back up your files in three different places. This is what professionals storing files and information recommend. Also be careful with your password. Some software will not allow you to retrieve and change your password if you forget it. I can vouch for this from personal experience!

Do not worry about grammar or spelling but do record the date for each entry. You should aim to get into the habit of writing in your journal regularly. It helps you get into a routine. So, writing it at the same time or place helps. You may at times have to set aside time for specific projects and aspects of your therapy. However, as soon as you have got into a routine you will find journaling an effortless, helpful, and natural part of your life. It is worth mentioning that some Apps have a built-in reminder that prompts you to regularly write in your journal. This is useful in helping you to develop a regular journal writing routine.

Personal Journal Sections
Apart from your general observations which you could record in a daily diary format, it can be useful to divide your journal into sections or headers.

1. Daily diary
2. Therapy journal (to record your therapy)
3. Specific problems & projects
4. Personal development, goals and plans
5. Gratitude journal
6. Business journal

All sections should include a review section.
It is good to review and look back, to see your former self.

Diary
You can use your personal journal as you would a daily diary simply to record your observations and interpretation of events. You may find that this could overlap with the sections below. So, you could just write the header for the relevant section above a particular entry.

Review Section (for all journal sections)
It's good to regularly review what you have written in your journal. There is no set period of time when you should do this. Just do it when it feels right for you, or when your therapy necessitates it. That said, it is best to get into a routine of regularly reviewing at least some sections in your diary. This can be done weekly, monthly or longer. Reviewing is helpful in evaluating what has happened, your progress to date and is a good tool for planning ahead and setting goals.

Therapy Journal
We will be using the Course Journal to support your therapy. However, you can also use your personal journal in which case your therapy journal section needs to meet certain requirements:
- Your therapy journal needs to be factual
- Your therapy journal needs to avoid too much focus on the negative
- Your therapy journal needs to be a positive force
- Your therapy journal needs to train your memory recall
- Your therapy journal needs to support your ongoing therapy
- Your therapy journal needs to record your therapy

Dream Journal

Use whenever you have a dream to write down. Keep a notebook or your journal by your bed and write down your dream immediately upon waking because dreams are easily forgotten.

There is no need to interpret the content of your dreams. Writing down the content of your dreams helps deal with bringing up repressed memories and emotions and can be useful in assisting with your therapy.

Historical Recall

This section should ideally be used in conjunction with types of analytical therapy involving memory recall and serves as a basis for assisting with the therapy in this course. I will give you full details in the Memory and Emotional Recall Therapy Section of this Anxiety Therapy Workbook, where you will be guided to use your Course Journal.

Specific Problems & Projects

Often in life we come up against a major problem or a difficult situation we must deal with. We become very worried about a feared outcome. Write down the worst-case scenario and then accept it. Fortunately, it rarely results in death! Take a few moments to fully appreciate how you will feel in this worst-case scenario. And really accept it. So, now that you have accepted the worst that can happen, you will find that you cease to worry about it. Now you should write down all the positive things you can do to make sure the worst-case scenario doesn't happen.

With a problem and an unresolved situation, you also write down the unresolved problem or unresolved situation in your personal journal and then write down all the possible options and solutions. Note down the possible end result of each possible course of action. When you have done this, you are best placed to work out your ideal solution to your problem or unresolved situation.

It can be helpful to write letters to people you have unresolved emotions with, but then don't send them.

Personal development, motivation, goals and plans

Without motivation you will not get far. And we know we are lacking motivation on some occasions. Normally, we are planning what we know is the right thing to do but feel ourselves lacking in motivation. It could be that you are seeking the motivation to continually use the therapy outlined in this course! Here is a journaling technique to give you the motivation you may need. Use it whenever you need to:

Pick a time when you will not be disturbed. Sit down with your personal journal in front of you, close your eyes and go ahead in time. The period of time varies with the thing you need to do. So, for example, let us say you have a mental, emotional or psychological problem you need to resolve. In other words, there is something inside of you but out of your control. Now go ahead one year in time and see that you have not stuck to your therapy program, and nothing has changed for you. Imagine where you are sitting in one year's time still feeling like you do now, but worse, because you realise you could be feeling much better by now! Imagine where you will be and how you would be feeling. Now write it down.

When you have written it down, clear your mind and close your eyes again and this time, imagine yourself one year ahead, but this time, see yourself as having persevered with the therapy, and you are feeling good, free of your problem and very proud of yourself. Open your eyes and write down your feelings should this be the outcome in one years' time.

Now understand how you will feel in one years' time as the result of each of the two outcomes above. And decide which path you would like to take. Based on the outcome of how you will feel in one years' time when you either you stuck to your therapy program, or you didn't.

Another example could be a diet or stopping smoking. Imagine how you will feel in a years' time if you have stayed with your diet or remained a non-smoker. Then imagine how you will feel in a years' time if you give up your diet or start smoking again.

The key thing is to go ahead in time and compare how you will feel as the result of doing something or not.

Gratitude journal
Getting into a habit of writing down something you are grateful for into your personal journal will help you view life in a more positive way and is especially helpful in tough times. You will find that being grateful for something, will attract more positive things into your life, there is always something in your life that you can be grateful for. It can be very small somethings to very large somethings! There are a considerable number of gratitude journal Apps available.

Business journal
Richard Branson keeps a business journal, starting right from his earliest days in business, according to his autobiography. It is a great tool for capturing ideas, making plans, and evaluating projects and setting goals. I will not go into any more detail here as its outside the scope of this course. Suffice it to say a separate business journal is a great tool, especially if you are self-employed or run your own business.

EXERCISE 3:

Go to your Course Journal and complete Exercise 3: Setting up your Personal Journal.

Now go to the Fast Help Section and find ways to get immediate help with your symptom/s.

5 Fast Help

"We tend to forget that happiness doesn't come as a result of getting something we don't have, but rather of recognising and appreciating what we do have."

Frederick Keonig

In this section I have documented various ways in which you can control negative thoughts, emotions and feelings relatively quickly.

Guided meditation/relaxation/hypnotherapy audio

This is a guided relaxation audio session that I have recorded where you can set time aside to relax, close your eyes and be guided through a relaxation session for around 35 minutes. Use it as often as you feel necessary. This has helped every client that I have given it to over many years. The effects are immediate and accumulative as you repeat the sessions over a period of time. You will need to set aside at least 35 minutes in a place where you can sit or lie down undisturbed. This can be just before you go to sleep at night if that suits you. If you fall asleep, the positive suggestions will still register in your mind and be effective.

EXERCISE 4:

Go to your Course Journal and listen to the **meditation, relaxation and hypnotherapy audio**. The link can be found in the Course Journal Appendix.

Stopping debilitating thoughts

The best way to gain control over your thoughts and in turn your emotions, is to practice meditation as taught in this course. It takes time, but you will gain control of your inner dialogue and be able to stop it when you need too. In the meantime, there are some techniques you can use below:

The techniques to stop your thoughts described in the meditation section of this course are equally effective outside your meditation session. So, I will go over them again here:

The Pause Button

Imagine, a pause button symbol represented by two parallel lines of the type found on a video or audio device and its corresponding remote control. Now think back on how you have used such a pause button to pause a film or movie you were watching. When you did this, you were able to see the film frozen on the screen. You were just left with a still image on the screen.

You can do the same with your thoughts. Simply, imagine an exceptionally large pause button symbol represented by two parallel lines superimposed over your thought. Now see your thought frozen just like when you paused a film on your TV phone or computer screen. Really concentrate on this pause button symbol superimposed over your thought, see it clearly in your mind's eye. This will stop your train of thoughts. If thoughts are frozen, they lose their power to continue. Their power is in their movement. Stop their movement and you have control over them. Repeat this procedure as often as you need too.

EXERCISE 5:

Go to your course journal and practice the pause button procedure on your unwanted thoughts as they travel through your mind. When you place the pause button over your thought, see the thought frozen in front of you like a clip of film.

The I am responsible affirmation!

Using the principle above that if thoughts are frozen, they lose their power to continue and if you stop their movement, you have control over them. A simple affirmation/statement which you repeat to yourself also works. This is "I am responsible". This means that you are saying to yourself "I am responsible for my thoughts". To start with, this will be very difficult to say. You will find yourself saying it through gritted teeth! However, if you persist and repeat this affirmation, it has the effect of freezing the movement of negative thoughts and so they lose their power, and you gain control of them. This is because this affirmation removes the power from a negative thought and its associated emotion.

EXERCISE 6:

Go to your Course Journal and try out the above "I am responsible" affirmation.

Another technique for stopping thoughts:

The fan
In your imagination or mind's eye, see a very large electric fan with its blades turning around in front of you. Now imagine walking into that fan, with its blades moving through the inside of your head scrambling and chewing up your thoughts. Take your time to vividly visualise this in your mind's eye. See those unwanted thoughts being shredded and broken up by the blades as they whirl around.

EXERCISE 7:
Go to your course journal and practice the fan procedure.

Further techniques for stopping thoughts:

- Without changing the content of your thoughts try to form them into a rhyme
- Make a song using the contents of your thoughts
- Think backward
- Think in a foreign language that is unfamiliar to you.
- Assign a number to each letter of each word of your thoughts, then add them up to determine the numerical result of your thoughts.
- Go through the multiplication tables
- Recite a prayer from a religion that is not your own
- Try to imitate the form of a well-known comic, using the contents of your thoughts as the material.

Walk in nature
Being in nature is a good way to relieve stress, anxiety, and mental health issues. Just 20 minutes in a place such as a park or beach can make a significant difference. Try to make this a regular occurrence. Once a week such as on weekends. I would, however, suggest much longer periods where perhaps you can get more deeply into nature. In times of stress this can be a truly healing experience. I can personally confirm this! Indeed, I have come across a number of cases where a person has been suffering from a severe debilitating mental illness and out of desperation, they have literally moved to live in a remote place in nature. Subsequently, they have seen their symptoms disappear and not return. This often works well in conjunction with getting in spirit or being inspired as described below.

EXERCISE 8:
Go to your Course Journal and complete the above "Walk in nature" exercise.

Get in spirit / inspired
We all need a purpose in life and so take your time to think and discover what inspires you. By that, I mean you need to find an activity, hobby or vocation that gives you an intense satisfaction. You could be living your dream like the lady who moved from the UK to set up and run a kite surfing school in a sunny foreign location to virtually eliminate her severe depression. But you do not necessarily need to go that far!
You simply need to find something to do, such as a hobby you love, something you like to do. Something that makes you feel good that you can immerse yourself in. It is probably something you are good at. Something or an activity you really look forward to. It is different for everyone. Think back in time, what have you enjoyed doing? What hobbies did you have? What hobby would you like to have? It could be an active one like hiking or a passive but creative one like drawing or painting. If you can enjoy creating something as a hobby, that also certainly works. Being involved in something that gives you pleasure and makes you feel good, being creative and doing something which gives you satisfaction is a great antidote to negative feelings and emotions. So, what will you do? Go to exercise 9 below and do it now!

EXERCISE 9:
Go to your Course Journal and complete the above "Get in spirit / inspired" exercise.

The Calm Technique
This is for when you need to stop a panic attack or to calm down and relax quickly. Stop what you are doing and take a big deep breath, hold it whilst counting silently from 1 to 3. And then slowly let it out. Repeat this for a total of 3 times. It is an amazingly simple quick and effective technique. I have broken it down into two steps below. So, try this right now!

Do the following 3 times consecutively:
- Take a very deep breath and then hold it as you slowly count from 1 to 3.
- At the count of 3 slowly let out all of your breath to completely empty your lungs.

EXERCISE 10:
Go to your Course Journal and complete the above "Calm Technique" exercise.

Emo-Trance

This method was developed by Dr Silvia Hartman and is described in her book "Oceans of Energy. The Patterns & Techniques of Emo-Trance, Volume 1", published in 2003. It is beyond the scope of this course to describe how it works. For this you will need to read her book! However, you just need to understand the technique for it to be effective. Just like you do not need to know how the inside of a television works in order to watch it!

Whilst Dr Hartman wrote a whole book on the subject, the core technique is very simple and effective in a matter of minutes. However, I must warn you, this technique will make no sense to the conscious rational part of you. But that is fine, because it does not need to. This is because it works at a deeper energetic subconscious level of your body. So, whilst when I describe the technique that you need to follow, you may think this is nonsense it doesn't make any sense, I am asking you to suspend your conscious judgment and just go along with it.

I have used Emo-Trance effectively on myself and with countless patients over a long period of time. I can vouch for its effectiveness in quickly removing painful emotions and feelings. I would suggest rehearsing the technique in your mind before you need to use it. So that you fully understand the sequence and so have the technique ready to use if you need it.

The Emo-Trance Technique

To start with you will have a feeling or emotion that you want to eliminate. For example, anger, guilt, panic, depression, anxiety apprehension, sadness, or fear. This could already have manifested in an area of your body and be expressing itself as a sick feeling or a tightness. It could also be a clear physical pain such as a migraine. It may not be instantly apparent as to where exactly in your body the feeling associated with your emotion or experience resides. So, the first thing to do is to identify exactly where in or on your body you notice the feeling associated with the negative emotion. So, for example if it is tension, where do you feel it? If it is anxiety, where in your body are you feeling it? Pinpoint the exact spot. If it is a feeling of nausea whereabouts exactly in your stomach, do you feel it? If its tension or pressure, zoom in and locate its centre. You get the idea. Do not think about it too much, just do it! Once you have located exactly where you are experiencing the feeling, focus in on the area, and observe its boundaries like it is a defined mass of energy which is producing the feeling you are experiencing.

Now, without thinking about the likely answer, ask yourself what colour the feeling/mass of energy is? There is no right or wrong answer. And you must not think about it. Just say the first colour that comes into your mind. Just ask the question and instantly say the first colour that comes into your mind. Remember what I said above, in that it will not make any sense to your rational conscious mind!

Now that you have identified the area, defined its mass, boundaries and colour. See it as a solid colour. This means that your feeling is now defined as something relatively solid with a mass and defined area. Now imagine breathing into this defined area and see your breath breaking it up. So, for example, if it is black like a lump of coal. See your breath breaking it up, as it breaks up see it disintegrating into grains of sand or vapour. In this example, grains of black sand or black vapour.

Now as this solid area breaks up into grains of sand or vapour, notice which way it is moving through your body from its defined area. Do not think about it, just notice which way it is moving out through your body. Notice which path it takes as it exits your body. There is no right or wrong way. Again, do not think about it, just observe.

Now keep breathing into the defined solid area and as you do this, keep visualising the solid defined area breaking up and the coloured sand or vapour moving away as it breaks up. Watch it moving through your body in its preferred direction which you already observed. As you keep doing this the feeling/emotion will slowly begin to disappear as this solid defined area breaks up and reduces. Keep breathing into the defined area, observing it breaking up into grains of sand or vapour and moving out through your body in its preferred direction. Eventually, the feeling will completely disappear.

If the feeling or negative emotion later returns, repeat the above exercise in its entirety, don't be surprised if any of the aspects are different such as the area where you locate the feeling in your body, colour and which way it wants to move through your body. This is because sometimes it is a bit like clearing through layer after layer. But your making progress as you work through each layer.

Here is a summary:

1. Locate and identify the specific area in your body where you are feeling the negative symptom, painful feeling or emotion. Observe its boundaries and see it as a defined mass of solid energy which is producing the feeling you are experiencing.
2. Now, without thinking about the likely answer, ask yourself what colour the feeling/mass of energy is?
3. Now see it as a solid colour.
4. Now imagine breathing into this solid colour and see your breath breaking up this defined area. As it breaks up, see it disintegrating into grains of sand or vapour in the colour you gave it.

5. Now as this solid area breaks up into grains of sand or vapour, notice which way it is moving to exit through your body from its defined area. Do not think about it, just notice which way it is moving out through your body. Notice which path it takes as it exits your body. There is no right or wrong way.
6. Keep breathing into the defined area whilst observing it breaking up into grains of sand or vapour and moving out through your body in its preferred direction. Until the feeling completely disappears.

As you may have noticed, Emo-Trance works at an energetic level within your body and as previously mentioned, makes no sense to your conscious mind. However, persevere because the results can be extremely rewarding.

EXERCISE 11:
Go to your Course Journal to memorise and complete the above Emo-Trance technique.

Externalisation and identification
Put simply, this involves externalising your negative feeling into a suitable activity. Either mentally or physically or both. Some people with mental health problems will already be doing this because their subconscious mind has discovered this mechanism to help relieve a painful emotion. You may have seen this in people who are workaholics, very keen sports people, people who dedicate themselves to helping a cause. This may not always be their motivation but often is.

EXERCISE 12:
Go to your Course Journal and write down what you can focus on in order to feel better.

Depression
Depression is a type of inward rage, where your feelings are directed back at you. this means you become withdrawn and inactive and consequently do not feel like doing anything.

The trick is to just do any small thing. Get involved in a small activity starting with just a small externalisation or activity to get your mental process moving outwardly. So, motivate yourself to do just one small thing right now and build on that.

EXERCISE 13:
If you are suffering from depression, go to your Course Journal and complete exercise 13.

Physical Exercise

When we get stressed, the body produces certain chemicals which place the body on alert. In the distant past of humanity, these chemicals were burnt up in action when we either ran from danger or fought it. This mostly does not happen now, so the stress chemicals stay in our body keeping us on alert, keeping us stressed and often making getting to sleep difficult. If you partake in exercise, by that I mean exercise that makes your heartbeat faster. This mimics the flight or fight response and burns up the stress chemicals in your body, enabling you to relax. What type of exercise am I writing about? Any exercise that gets your heart beating faster, such as a run or a swim, exercise bike, jogging on the spot or visit to the gym. This exercise to get your heart beating faster could just be for 10 minutes. So, such an activity after a stressful day at work may work wonders!

EXERCISE 14:

Go to your Course Journal to complete this physical exercise.

How to stop worrying

If you have a problem that needs solving and is causing you to worry, get it out of your mind and write it down in your journal or on a sheet of paper. Next write down all the possible scenarios and possibilities. Then write down the worst-case scenario and accept it for a few moments. Then write out what positive things you can do to avoid the worst-case scenario. You cannot then worry about the worst-case scenario anymore because you have accepted it. You are now working positively towards a solution.

EXERCISE 15:

Go to your Course Journal to complete the exercise which will help you to stop worrying.

Expressing Gratitude

Using your journal or workbook to record what you are grateful for each day is a well-documented, tried and tested way of making yourself feel better. You do not necessarily need a journal but, its best to use one for long term benefits. It is a simple principle, it just involves thinking what you can be grateful for right now. It can be anything from a loving partner to a sunny day or a nice flower. No matter how bad you think things are, I can absolutely guarantee you can find something to be grateful for.

Being grateful focuses your mind on a positive aspect of your life. Expressing gratitude, will attract more positive feelings and events into your life too. Importantly, it will also direct your chain of thoughts down a more positive road thus, attracting more positivity into your life. Therefore, making you feel better and uplifting your mood. Try this first thing in the morning to set yourself up for the day. I would strongly advise not listening too or watching the news or reading about the news first thing in the morning. It is much better to read something positive and uplifting instead, if you're aiming to have a positive mood for the day! Some people also use a gratitude stone. It is simply a nice small smooth pebble, that you can put in your pocket for the day. Every time you notice it in your pocket it reminds you what you decided to be grateful for that day. Try this regularly for a week, what have you got to lose?

There is also another way of expressing gratitude which you may find easier to do on a regular basis. This exercise is performed last thing at night before going to bed and is very simple and easy to do and leaves you with a feel-good factor before going to sleep. Simply write down three good things that happened to you that day. They can be very small things like appreciating a flower or, a smile from a stranger to hugely significant things like something or somebody exciting coming into your life.

EXERCISE 16:
Go to your Course Journal and complete the gratitude exercise over the next 30 days.

Don't take yourself too seriously!
We are all guilty of taking ourselves too seriously, it causes all manner of problems in relating to other people. Next time you find yourself getting impatient or over thinking something, tell yourself to stop taking yourself too seriously! Read the story below and try to apply the principal when appropriate and in a situation, which demands it. You can practice it when your next held up in a queue, I often do!

Remember rule number 6
Two prime ministers are sitting in a room discussing affairs of state. Suddenly a man bursts in, apoplectic with fury, shouting and stamping and banging his fist on the desk.

The resident prime minister admonishes him: "Peter" he says, "kindly remember Rule Number 6," whereupon Peter is instantly restored to complete calm, apologises and withdraws.

The politicians return to their conversation, only to be interrupted yet again twenty minutes later by a hysterical woman gesticulating wildly, her hair flying.

Again, the intruder is greeted with the words: "Marie, please remember Rule Number 6." Complete calm descends once more, and she too withdraws with a bow and an apology.

When the scene is repeated for a third time, the visiting prime minister addresses his colleague: "My dear friend, I've seen many things in my life, but never anything as remarkable as this. Would you be willing to share with me the secret of Rule Number 6?"

"Very simple," Replies the resident prime minister. "Rule Number 6 is 'Don't take yourself so goddamn seriously".

"Ah," says his visitor, "that is a fine rule."

After a moment of pondering, he inquires, "And what, may I ask, are the other rules?"

"There aren't any."

From "The Art of Possibility" by Rosamund and Benjamin Zander.

EXERCISE 17: Go to your Course Journal to use the "Don't take yourself too seriously" story above.

Paradoxical Intention

You should never use Paradoxical Intention if you are suffering from psychotic depression. However, if you have any suicidal ideas or are suffering from any type of depression, consult your doctor before using Paradoxical Intention and then make sure you are under medical supervision. Paradoxical Intention is a powerful therapeutic technique for combatting neurosis, phobias, and anxiety. Paradoxical Intention means that you try or wish to happen the very thing that you fear. This is an effective and proven technique used in Psychotherapy and Logotherapy.

Dr Hans O Gertz, the clinical director of Connecticut Valley Hospital found that 88% of all patients who were suffering from obsessive-compulsive conditions recovered or made a considerable improvement. In Russia, Prof A M Swjadustch claimed that Paradoxical Intention was used in his hospital with success in the treatment of phobias and anticipatory anxiety neurosis.

When a person is trying to make happen the thing they most fear, they are inverting their attention, therefore diverting their attention from causing the event to happen again. Paradoxical Intention gives you the capacity to detach yourself not only from the world but also from yourself. This ability provides a powerful therapeutic technique for combating neurosis, phobias, and anxiety etc.

Paradoxical Intention works very well with anticipatory anxiety where you are anxious about something happening, phobias and obsessive-compulsive disorders where you feel compelled to obsessively do something.

Once we associate anxiety or fear with an "event" that could be anything or something that has happened, you are likely to become fearful that the "event" will reoccur or happen again. This is called anticipatory anxiety and helps bring on a reoccurrence of the "event". It is also possible to have a fear of fear itself. In other words, fear of being becoming frightened. Anxiety is fear spread thinly, so you may experience anxiety about becoming anxious again.

As stated above, anticipatory anxiety tends to occur when you fear the reoccurrence of an event. For example, the recurrence of the symptoms of a panic attack. The fact that you are fearing a reoccurrence of an event tends to make happen precisely what you were worrying or in fear about. Therefore, you enter into a vicious cycle whereby the memory of the event about which you were anxious, creates a fear that it will reoccur. The fear that it will reoccur provokes its reoccurrence, you then re-experience its reoccurrence which reenforces the fear or anxiety that it will happen again, this means it is more likely that it will happen again, hence the aforementioned vicious cycle.

So, we can use Paradoxical Intention to break this vicious cycle. Paradoxical Intention inverts your intention in that by trying to make the feared event happen, you are diverting your intention from causing the event to happen again. In other words, the wind is taken out of your anticipatory anxiety. You stop fuelling your symptom. If you're fighting your symptom, you are fuelling it! Paradoxical Intention is best used with humour for maximum effect. Humour helps with self detachment and transcendence of oneself.

Using Paradoxical Intention reverses your attitude, in as much that your fear or anxiety is replaced by a paradoxical wish so the mental energy fuelling the anxiety or fear is removed.

First some simple examples are called for:

Trying to pass an exam or driving test. The more anxious or stressed you are, the harder it's going to be to pass. People often fail because they were trying too hard to pass. I only passed my driving test because less than halfway into my test I was convinced that I had failed. As soon as I became convinced I had failed, I didn't care anymore. So, I just drove normally as if I was driving with a friend. It turned out the mistakes I had made were not critical and by subsequently relaxing through the remainder of the test enabled me to pass.

Another simple example which you may relate too, is when you are unable to get to sleep, the more you try to get to sleep the harder it is. The moment you stop trying and maybe even try to stay awake, the more likely it will be that you will fall asleep. If you wake up in the night, it's best not to look at the time because you will be conscious of how much time you have left in bed and may start trying to get to sleep. This means it is more likely that you will not be able to get back to sleep!

An example of unintentional use of Paradoxical Intention is given in Professor Victor's Frankl's book "The Will to Meaning": In a high school play one of the characters was a stutterer. So, they gave the part to a student who actually stuttered in real life. However, the student who actually stuttered in real life, had to give up the acting role because when standing on stage trying to stutter for his role, he was unable to stutter. Therefor he had to be replaced by another actor.

Fear that people will laugh at you: Try and make people laugh at you, make fun of yourself.

Fear of eating in public: Go out for a meal and tell yourself you are going to try and get noticed perhaps in a hilarious way.

If you force yourself to do something you are afraid off, it has the reverse effect. If you can also add humour and or exaggeration, that makes Paradoxical intention more effective.

So, try and make what you fear happen. If you exaggerate the result, it will become humorous. For example, if you have an obsessive-compulsive disorder whereby you are consciously washing your hands. Set up a schedule in your diary to wash your hands maybe every couple of hours, so the whole exercise becomes exaggerated and thus becomes humorous and ridiculous.

To help you gain an understanding of how to apply Paradoxical Intention, here are some further examples of case histories using Paradoxical Intention as reported by Professor Victor Frankl in his book "The Doctor and the Soul, from Psychotherapy to Logotherapy":

Mrs Anna H. 40 years old. Symptom: Washing compulsion since the age of 5, often stayed up to 5am due to chronic perfectionism. severe compulsive repetition requiring her to get up at 4am in order to attend therapy at 12 midday. Paradoxical Intention Therapy sessions involved the patient learning to wish everything would be as dirty as possible. The patient was discharged from hospital and made a dramatic recovery.

Horst S. 17-year-old boy. Speech disturbance in the form of stuttering. Began four years previously at school when classmates laughed at him when he was reciting in class. Dr Eisenman the treating physician succeeded in getting him to say to himself, whenever the stuttering anxiety gripped him: "Oh, I'm afraid that I'll stutter on a "b" or an "a!" Well, today I think I will stutter through the entire alphabet for a change!". He was later able to resume classroom recitation free of any speech difficulty.

A man visited the neurological department of a hospital suffering from severe anxiety attacks unable to go out unless his wife accompanied him. He could not ride on a bus and was haunted by a fear that he would collapse and die. When seen by Dr Kurt Kocoourek he was caught in an overpowering fear, with intense excitement and copious perspiring. And so was scheduled for admission to hospital.

Dr Kurt Kocoourek treated him with paradoxical intention. The doctor's advice was to start telling himself "Now I shall go out onto the street and try and collapse". After two psychotherapeutic sessions he managed to sit in a crowded café. At first, he felt some anxiety but then he told himself: "now let's collapse, inviting himself to do so. Afterwards he was free from fear. Later he attended his child's overcrowded school parent teacher conference, this was previously what he had most dreaded until now. Before leaving, he jokingly told himself: "now I'm going to the school building to die. What a beautiful funeral it will be." On the same day the patient went to his club, usually he went there with great anxiety, but this time he went in order that he "should faint away from heat stroke in the stuffy room, and for the sake of getting asphyxiated by the fumes of the stove". However, this time there were no symptoms. Now when he speaks of paradoxical intention, he laughs heartily and says, "this is fun, it really worked". He now forgets to apply paradoxical intention for he does not need it anymore.

W.S aged 35, developed the phobia that he would die from a heart attack as well as a phobic fear of not being able to get to sleep. When Dr Gerz, the treating physician, instructed him to go ahead and try as hard as possible to make his heart beat fast and die of a heart attack right on the spot, he laughed and replied; "Doc, I'm trying hard but I can't do it." Dr. Gerz instructed him to go ahead and try and die from a heart attack each time anticipatory anxiety troubled him. When the patient began laughing about his neurotic symptoms, humour entered and helped him put a distance between himself and his neurosis. The patient left the doctor's office relieved with instructions to "die at least three times a day of a heart attack and instead of trying to get to sleep, he should try to remain awake. The patient was seen 3 days later symptom free.

This case of successful use of paradoxical intention comes from Dr Godfryd Kacanowski, past clinical director of Ontario Hospital in Canada. A good-looking well-groomed career woman had been suffering for 15 years from constant tension, anxiety, periodical depression, feelings of inadequacy and panic attacks. She complained that her life was miserable in spite of the external appearance of success. She had more than an average growth of bodily hair and said that her greatest fear was that hair might start growing on her face. This fear never left her. She became so frightened that she was unable to look in the mirror except from a considerable distance. She said that she would die the moment she saw hair growing on her face. Doctor Kacanowski told her to wish that one hair would grow on her cheek. The woman nearly fainted. She looked at him as if she was seeing a monster. 10 minutes later he was able to lead her to a wall mirror. For the first time in years, she looked closely in the mirror, and she chose the place on her cheek where she wished one hair to grow. During the next session she chose a place on her other cheek. For a long time, she could not see the humour in this situation, but she had courage. Finally, her fear that hair would cover her face was greatly alleviated.

To summarise:

A person suffering from a phobia usually tries to avoid the situation in which their anxiety arises, whilst a person who has an obsessive-compulsive symptom tries to suppress and thus fight their threatening ideas. In either case the result is a strengthening of the symptoms. Yet if the person can stop fleeing or fighting their symptoms but on the contrary, even exaggerate them, the symptoms disappear. You can therefore see that the person is reacting with a flight or fight behaviour pattern. Humour used with exaggeration helps this process of detachment from the symptom.

Make a note of your symptom and decide what exactly you fear.

Think about how you could try and make what you fear happen.

Think how you can exaggerate your fear so that it becomes ridiculous and therefore humorous. Humour helps with detachment and transcendence.

Finally, Paradoxical Intention can be hard to understand because it seems counter intuitive. It is, however, an established technique in Psychotherapy and Logotherapy. And, most importantly, Paradoxical Intention will work even if you firmly believe it won't.

EXERCISE 18:

Now go to your course journal and complete the Paradoxical Intention exercise.

6 Introduction to Meditation

"Your worst enemy cannot harm you as much as your own thoughts unguarded".
Buddha

What is Meditation?

There are different types of meditation. But generally, meditation uses techniques to slow down and even stop the constant chatter of the mind and gain control over one's mental processes, thus achieving a more relaxed state. Meditation has been practiced in various forms for thousands of years.

True Meditation is not about concentration, although concentration can be used as an aid to learn meditation. Meditation is about being fully present in the moment with a heightened awareness.

Many of the meditation techniques taught today are in fact methods to train the mind to slow down to a state of thoughtless awareness. The state of thoughtless awareness is in fact true meditation. You can nevertheless obtain benefits soon after starting your meditation practice as you begin to gain control over your mind and start to relax and de-stress.

Meditation is about getting to know your true self whilst experiencing deep relaxation. It has been used in schools, businesses, prisons and universities. Many celebrities practice meditation including Jennifer Aniston, Arnold Schwarzenegger, Camron Diaz, Russell Brand, Jerry Seinfeld, Katy Perry, Sky Ferreira, Sheryl Crow and Ellen DeGeneres.

Two Stages of Meditation

Essentially there are two stages to meditation and depending on the type of meditation used and how you practice it, you may only predominantly experience stage 1.

Stage 1: Mindfulness

Mindfulness meditation practice can include focusing on an object, staying in the present, paying attention, being non-judgemental, focusing on your breathing and or your body. Being present in your body and observing your feelings. It can also include practicing Yoga and Yoga movements.

Stage 2: Thoughtless Awareness

Called transcendence in Transcendental / Vedic meditation. Otherwise called the still mind, beyond the thinking process, and the silent mind. When stage 2 is achieved you can still practice mindfulness/thought control during your everyday life. So, stage 1 and 2 can be practiced side by side. The term transcendence can also be used to describe a special state of consciousness that can be attained during meditation that is difficult to put into words. It can be experienced as a sense of euphoria where time ceases to exist, your sense of your body is lost, and you experience a profound sense of connection to all that is and will ever be. People who have been meditating for many years (and sometimes only a few months) often say that this state of special consciousness is obtained infrequently and may only last for minutes or seconds. Nevertheless, it has a lasting positive effect on their wellbeing. I have frequently experienced a similar state myself and would describe it as a sense of timelessness and disconnection from my body but, being aware and connected to all that is and all that can be. Well, I did say it is difficult to describe, didn't I? It must be experienced! The mind is like the ocean in that your thoughts are the waves and the ocean is the still mind beneath. Like the waves that sit upon the surface and form only a very small part of the ocean, your thoughts represent only a very small part of your mind. Essentially, your thoughts could represent just 1% of your mind. However, most people believe they are only their thoughts!

So, you will be pleased to learn that your worries, fears, anxiety, negative emotions and the like, are not really you. They are not your true self; they are the false in you. Meditation gives you access to the silent part of your mind, where you can observe this false part of you. You can observe your thoughts and as you develop a sense of self separation, you are able to gain control over your thoughts and in turn your negative emotions.

In an earlier section we discussed the conscious and subconscious mind. So, where does meditation fit in? To the conscious and subconscious mind, we can add the superconscious mind, otherwise called your higher self, where the silent but aware part I mentioned earlier resides. To this we can add your Ego. The thinking part of you, the part which you think is you, where your thoughts come from, and you think you are your thoughts don't you? We can place the Ego in the conscious mind.

The term superconscious mind otherwise called your higher self, would suggest a more powerful and resourceful part of you. This is certainly the case. The ultimate aim of meditation is to access this part of your mind. From there you can relax more deeply, get rid of stress and recharge your energy quickly. When you are aware from your superconscious mind you are in a state of self-separation. You are separate from your ego and conscious thinking self and so you are able to observe your thoughts. Especially the negative ones. You gain a control over your thoughts so that you can stop yourself worrying, for example. From this separated state you can also observe your feelings and emotions. You will come to realise they are separate from your higher self, you will see that these negative feelings are not the real you, they are the false in you. And what do we do with something we discover is false? We discard it! You will do the same with those negative feelings and emotions. Likewise, you will gain control and disregard the thoughts you would rather not have.

From a spiritual point of view, it is said that your higher self has a much better access to the creator of all that is, or God. Or whomever or whatever higher force you feel comfortable with.

Benefits of meditation

Observed benefits include:

Help with mental health problems

Lower blood pressure

Reduced stress levels

Help with sleep

Help with post-traumatic stress disorder

Help with addictions

Reduced worry

Increased focus

Better relaxation

Increased energy

Feeling happier

Additionally, considering that stress can cause all manner of health problems, by reducing stress, the benefits of meditation can be multiplied many times.

TYPES OF MEDITATION

Meditation for focusing on a particular outcome
For example, expressing love and kindness to everyone or solving a particular problem.

Focusing on the body
This includes progressive relaxation and scanning the body.

Mindfulness Meditation
This involves suspending all judgment and focusing on the present rather than the past or the future. Mindfulness is present in most kinds of meditation when for example, you are focusing on your body, your breath or a guided meditation. Mindfulness meditation can also be practiced outside of your daily meditation practice. For example, whilst you are going about your daily activities your mind is focused on the present with all critical thinking and judgment suspended. More about this later when I explain meditation practice.

Yoga
Some forms of Yoga combine meditation such as Kundalini which is a physically active form of meditation that combines movements with deep breathing and mantras. You usually need to learn this with a teacher but can subsequently practice at home.

Contemplation Meditation
Contemplation meditation involves contemplating something. The most common contemplation subject is God, as is the case in Raj Yoga.

Zen Meditation
Zen meditation, sometimes called Zazen is a form of meditation that can be part of Buddhist practice. This is best learnt with a teacher because this kind of meditation involves specific steps and postures. The goal is to find a comfortable position, focus on breathing, and mindfully observe one's thoughts without judgment.

Again, this form of meditation is like mindfulness meditation but requires more discipline and practice. People may be drawn to this type of meditation if they are seeking a spiritual path.

Transcendental Meditation
Transcendental Meditation is based on the Vedic knowledge that goes back many thousands of years. Vedic Meditation was introduced into the western world as

Transcendental Meditation in the 1950's by Mararishi Mahesh Yogi. It became well known in 1967 when the Beatles learnt meditation with Mararishi. Since then, a significant number of celebrities have and are currently practicing Transcendental Meditation and actively recommend it. Transcendental Meditation uses a silent mantra to quieten the mind. This mantra is given by a Transcendental Meditation teacher along with tuition and instructions. Participants practice for two 20-minute sessions a day.

Meditation as taught in this course
We are aiming for all the benefits of meditation I have written about so far. Which include reducing stress, eliminating worry and becoming calmer with increasing energy. But as the title of this course suggests, I will be guiding you through specific techniques to help with any mental health issues you need to resolve. Some if not most of these meditation techniques are taken from the different types of meditation. Some are unique for the purpose of helping with a mental health problem or stress. However, this meditation technique is recommended even if you are perfectly fine and just want to achieve a state of continued wellbeing.

I was fortunate in that the first book I ever read on meditation was by the late Barry Long, a well-known meditation guru and spiritual leader of his time. His foundation carries on. Barry wrote that the purpose of meditation was to find the state of stillness within you and after stillness the secret is self-separation. He also said that the purpose of meditation is to get to know yourself… your real self. Now, please don't confuse the state of stillness with being vacant and unaware. Far from it, you will be more aware. Imagine a large lion poised, still, silent, and alert ready to pounce on its prey. 100 percent aware. That is the kind of still and aware I am writing about. Look into your pet's eyes, they have no internal dialogue going through their heads like you do, but; they are very much aware and able to act in an instant.

Self-separation which at first you will experience very briefly in fleeting moments is achieved when you realise that there are two parts of you. The observed and the observer. For example, in meditation when you are silently observing your body, there is the part doing the observing and then there is your body. The aim is to silently observe, your body, breath or whatever you decide to observe or be aware of. This will depend on the type of meditation you are practicing. The aim is to stop the constant internal dialogue of your mind. Starting out, this is very difficult if not impossible. So, we focus the mind for example, on a mantra, on breathing, on different parts of the body, guided meditation, or an external object. However, frequently you will find your thoughts intrude and off you go on a stream of thoughts. Then again and again you realise this is happening, you stop your thoughts and you go back to your meditation/mantra. This process is repeated frequently, but each time you notice and stop your thoughts intruding, you gain a degree of self-separation. As you practice you get better at noticing and stopping your thoughts, especially the negative and bad ones! The aim is to make the thoughtless periods longer and longer. Indeed, as you practice, these periods do get longer. Persistence is the key here!

The aim is to become master of your own mind. The part of your mind we are referring to here is your conscious mind. The part you think is you! Within this part resides mechanical worry, anger, hate, arguing, envy, judging others, fear, regret, and other feelings. Your mind currently controls you and may overwhelm you with negative emotions. So, you see, the conscious mind itself is the problem. Yet we cannot use the mind to defeat the mind. Therefore, it is important to use the right meditation technique and why some meditation methods fail in this endeavour. The more you meditate using the correct meditation technique which I will show you, the more you will gain control of your mind, so negative emotions will begin to go.

Meditation is a lifestyle choice, it is an everyday commitment of at least 20 minutes. I say commitment but, it is not a chore, it is a good experience, you will look forward to it and if you miss a day, you will feel like you're missing something. That is what people who practice meditation usually say and I can confirm it through personal experience! The best times to meditate are in the morning around breakfast time and in the evening around the time you get home from work or after your evening meal. It does not matter too much, but it is best to get into a regular routine. However, I have found that practicing meditation very close to bedtime when I am tired hinders meditation, as I am fighting off falling asleep and my brain is heading towards the dreaming state.

When you first start out you really should have a daily meditation whether you feel like it all not. But not to worry, you will soon be effortlessly settling into an easy routine. This is because you are building a new habit. Let me tell you something about habits. It takes approximately 30 days or 4 weeks to get a new habit. You focus on doing something for 30 days or so, and then your subconscious mind takes over and you do it automatically. Let me give you an example. Imagine that you have a fridge in your kitchen, it has been there in the same place for a long time. Then all of a sudden you need to get a new fridge, but it won't fit in the same place, so you have to put your freezer where your fridge was and your fridge where your freezer was. It is a certainty that for the first week you are going to keep going to the freezer without thinking about it when you need milk for your tea or a filling for your sandwich! And so on!

Another example of how we build habits is called for. Imagine you go to your dentist and your dentist tells you that you need to start cleaning your teeth in the morning as well as at night. Now, you know some mornings you are going to forget! So, you write a note to yourself on the bathroom mirror which says clean teeth. So, every morning you are reminded and clean your teeth. Now, imagine after 30 days when it has become a habit and you no longer need a note to remind you, you go back to your dentist and your dentist tells you for some reason, you must stop cleaning your teeth in the morning! When you get home, you will have to write another note to stick on the bathroom mirror which says, "DO NOT CLEAN TEETH"! Otherwise, you will clean them without realising you are doing it in the morning without thinking about it!

The next section moves on to meditation practice. I have called the meditation in the next section Altered State Meditation but, essentially, it is Vedic meditation, based on the ancient Vedic knowledge like Transcendental Meditation. Of all the different meditations, it is the easiest meditation to learn and master, the one that requires no concentration or effort, and is the easiest to practice. This is, therefore, the meditation you should start right now and continue to practice as you continue through this course working on your therapy.

EXERCISE 19:
Now go to your Course Journal to complete the quiz for this section.

7 Meditation Practice

"Meditation is not a way of making your mind quiet. It's a way of entering into the quiet that's already there – buried under the 50,000 thoughts the average person thinks every day". Deepak Chopra

Altered State Meditation

I have called this meditation, Altered State Meditation. It is, however, primarily based on Vedic Meditation which uses a mantra to effortlessly calm and still the mind. Vedic meditation comes from the ancient Vedic knowledge going back many thousands of years. No concentration is required and so this is an extremely easy meditation to learn. This means the desired results come much quicker with considerably less effort compared to most other types of meditation.

Vedic meditation is a simple silent natural effortless technique. There is no concentration or control of the mind required. Absolutely no philosophy or religion is involved. There is nothing to believe in and apart from allocating time for your meditation, there is no need for a change in your lifestyle. The technique will even work if you are sceptical.

To explain how it works, it helps to use the analogy similar to the one I used in the previous section. The mind is like the ocean. By that, I mean that there are waves on the top and a vast deep, silent calm expanse of water beneath. The waves on the surface of the ocean represent your conscious mind/ego with its thoughts racing along constantly at a fast pace one after the other, often putting a lot of pressure on you. However, the ocean below is vast, large, quiet, and still, just like most of your mind beneath your thoughts. You do not realise this because you currently have little or no access to it.

Vedic meditation is a simple natural effortless technique to help the part of the mind represented by the waves above, to slow down and eventually, to stop for short periods of time. Thus, giving you access to the vast still part of you, the real and larger part of you which I previously labelled as your higher self or super-consciousness. This whole process involves a deep relaxation which is often deeper than that experienced during sleep. Therefore, stress, anxiety, post-traumatic stress disorder and high blood pressure are considerably alleviated. I have previously mentioned additional benefits in the Introduction to Meditation Section.

At a minimum, you will need to practice this meditation once a day for 20 minutes. Ideally, you should have two 20-minute sessions a day every day, so this is a lifestyle choice. It is however, worth the rewards both mentally and physically. Ideally, your first meditation should be after you have had breakfast or at least some sort of activity and so are wide awake and alert. The second session should be after work or early evening but, not so late that you are getting tired as bedtime approaches. For most people this may be between 5 and 8pm. You will find that you look forward to your meditation and if you miss it, you really notice it!

Your mantra

Before you can start your meditation practice, you will need to select your mantra. A great deal has been written about mantras. However, ultimately for our purpose, a mantra is simply a word which when repeated influences the human mind. Whatever mantra you select it should have no meaning to you, otherwise, your mind will latch on to the meaning during your meditation and as it is our aim to still the mind, that is not what you want.

The thinking part of your mind represented by the waves in my analogy above, is naturally and effortlessly drawn and attracted to your mantra. It becomes entrained by it and thus, starts to slow down and initially stops for noticeably short periods of time. These periods get longer with practice. Relaxation is therefore experienced. This technique is different to the difficult concentration and effort methods used by some other meditation techniques.

Mantra selection

There are a number of different mantra's you could use. For the Vedic meditation you are learning here, it is traditional to use the Vedic Bija or seed mantras. There are around 35 of them in use today. Here are 4 examples.

Shrim

Pronounced: Shur – ream
shur as when you say shirt and ream as in a quantity of paper or a great amount such as in "reams of information".

Krim
Pronounced: Key-ream Key as in key for a lock and ream as in a quantity of paper or a great amount such as in "reams of information".

Hirim
Pronounced: He – ream
He as in he is my brother and ream as in a quantity of paper or a great amount such as in "reams of information".

Shiama
Pronounced: She – arm – a
she as in she is my wife, arm as in my hand is attached to my arm and a as in, I have a cat

Im Na Mah
This is an advanced Vedic mantra with a specific tonality. There are three parts to it. The First part: is "IM" spelt IM as in I'm going to start meditating now.

The second part is spelt "NA" and sounds like slang for "no"

The third part spells MAH and sounds like slang for "mother"

It is expressed with three syllables with the first being the highest.

It is essential that you listen to the accompanying audio showing you how to use and pronounce this mantra.

I would suggest that you use this mantra and see how you get on. I have made a recording to guide you through how to use this mantra.

How to use your mantra
After saying your mantra out aloud whilst initially practicing pronouncing it, you should then only repeat your mantra silently in your mind, not out aloud. When you are repeating your mantra during your meditation, it is not necessary to keep repeating it in the exact form in which you learnt it. You can certainly aim to start your meditation repeating it in its exact form but, as you progress with your meditation using your mantra, its repetition can end up as only a vague memory of its original form. You may find that you continue again as you originally learnt it as you progress through your meditation and then it fades again into a vague memory. Feel free to let this happen. So, you have started your meditation and are now repeating your mantra silently focusing on how it sounds in your mind. You will find that a thought comes in, initially you will find that a whole train of thoughts come in. When you notice that thoughts

have intruded, go back to the mantra and move back to focus on your mantra. You may find that you have thoughts and the mantra both running at the same time. When you notice this, gently favour your mantra over the thought so the thought fades. Do not forcefully try and stop your thoughts. When you notice thoughts, simply move back to the mantra or gently favour the mantra over the thoughts if you notice both are running at the same time.

When repeating your mantra, I want you to notice the gap in between, by that, I mean I want you to notice the silence in between your mantra each time you repeat it. An ancient Zen observation says that it is the silence between the notes that creates the music. Music without any pauses or silent spaces would be one long note making music impossible. So, notice the beginning and end of your mantra each time you repeat it and the gap in between your repetition of your mantra. When you start your meditation, the gap/silence between each repetition of your mantra maybe barely noticeable. However, as you progress through your meditation you may notice the silence between the repetition of your mantra getting longer as you slow down and relax more into your meditation, until you eventually stop in the gap and silence between your mantra with no thoughts present.

So, as you practice, you may notice that the mantra has stopped, and all thoughts have stopped. Then a thought comes in and so you start the mantra again. This brief period of no thought or mantra is where you have transcended into a higher greatly beneficial state of consciousness. It needs to last for only seconds for you to get long term benefits. No thoughts and only your mantra is also very beneficial.

Make sure you memorise this section on how to use your mantra fully in preparation for your meditation.

Stress and releasing negative emotions
If you notice any negative or painful emotions, and or stress arising just keep with your mantra and allow the negative emotion/feeling to dissolve in its own time. Do not start thinking about the negative feeling. Just notice the feeling as you repeat the mantra. The negative feeling is not the real you, so it will dissolve as you just notice it and repeat the mantra alongside it. Be patient, It will dissolve. If you find thoughts intruding, the same rule applies in that you favour your mantra over the thought.

You will find that stress will naturally be released during your meditation. That is one of the main benefits of this type of meditation. Most of us have a lot of stress and tension to release. A good analogy would be to see stress in the body like a screw that has been turned tighter and tighter. Now in meditation, it is slowly turning the other way and unwinding losing its tension, as it releasees your stress. Think how tight your muscles get under stress and this analogy takes on a reality! That is what a massage does, it releases tension created by stress in your body.

When stress is encountered during meditation prior to release, it can prompt a thought. Not necessarily a thought about the stress, but just what seems like a random thought. That means your mantra or thoughtless state is interrupted. You may not be aware that stress has prompted the thought, but that is not important. Just go back to your mantra, or if you are already repeating your mantra, just gently favour your mantra over the thought as I have described above.

MEDITATION PRACTICE

The meditation session comprises of 3 parts or modules. Part 1 the relaxation introduction, part 2 the meditation itself which takes up most of the session. Part 3 is the final two minutes used to gradually bring you back to everyday life. We also have the option of using these last few minutes for a calming and energising visualisation exercise.

Before starting:

Firstly, you need to find a place where you will not be disturbed, and you can sit comfortably. You should be able to sit comfortably in an upright position. Avoid lying down. There is no need to sit in a lotus-like position as you may have seen in photographs of people meditating. That is how people sit in the eastern countries where the photographs were taken. They find it comfortable sitting that way because that is their normal sitting position. If that is not your normal sitting position, you will find it uncomfortable. If you are uncomfortable, it will be difficult for you to meditate. If you find it difficult to find time alone, you may have to get creative like parking somewhere in your car on your way home from work. If practicing at home, just let your family know what you are doing and ask them not to disturb you for 20 minutes. When you get into a routine it will be much easier. So, you have a chair or seat, and you have a place where hopefully, you will not be disturbed. Make sure you are warm enough.

I would suggest setting a timer for 20 minutes with a tone that is soft and not too startling or loud, especially if you need to be doing something immediately after your meditation. There is a free meditation App you can download on your phone called Insight Timer.

EXERCISE 20:
Now go to your Course Journal and listen to the audio recording titled **Introduction to meditation with the IM NA MAH mantra**. Only after you have finished working through this exercise should you move on to the next exercise, 21.

EXERCISE 21:
Now that you have completed exercise 20 and have become familiar with your mantra, go to your Course Journal and listen to the **guided altered state meditation audio**. Should you wish to use them the printed instructions are below:

Altered State Meditation instructions for you to memorise should you wish to do so:
Before proceeding you should by now have memorised and practiced your chosen Mantra and have fully memorised and understood the procedures outlined in this section up to this point. Remember, you should repeat your mantra silently in your mind, not out aloud.

Ok, so you are now sitting somewhere with a comfortable temperature. You are comfortable and you will not be disturbed. You have set your timer and you are good to start meditating! After your sessions regularly review the instructions again in this section considering your ongoing experience.

1 Relaxation Introduction Module
Before you start your meditation, it is advisable to spend a small amount of time to slowdown and give yourself a bit of space between your daily activities and relax. The following progressive relaxation sequence is easy to remember and practice. Simply start at the top of your body and slowly work down. Just tense and relax each part in sequence from head to toe. It should take no more than two or three minutes.

1. Sit upright on your chair with your head erect with your feet a few inches apart.
2. Your hands on your thighs, held loosely together on your lap or resting gently by your side.
3. Look upward slightly and fix your eyes on a spot either real or imaginary in front of you.
4. Tell yourself you are going to silently count to 3 and on the count of 3, your eyes will close, and you will begin to relax.
5. Now count to 3 and let your eyes close.
6. Start your relaxation by fixing your attention on your feet. Begin with your toes, curl your toes, and let them go, notice the sensation as they relax. Let the relaxation rise up into both of your feet. Notice the sensation in your feet. Tense

and relax your legs below your knees. Then allow the relaxation to flow up into your calf muscles. Take your time to sense the feeling in your calf muscles.

7. Let the relaxation rise up over your thighs and let both of your legs relax.
8. Now fix your attention on your stomach, relax every muscle, every nerve and every fibre in your stomach as your stomach rests.
9. Now focus on your chest, notice how each deep breath is relaxing you more and more.
10. Now place your attention on your hands and your arms. Begin with your fingers, tightly close your fingers, pause, then open them and feel your hands relax. Let that relaxation rise up through your hands, wrists, forearms and upper arms. Take your time, notice the physical sensations as your hands, wrists, forearms and upper arms progressively relax.
11. Let that relaxation sweep across your shoulders, notice any areas of tension or tightness in your shoulders, and let it go.
12. Let the relaxation rise up the back of your head, across the top of your head and down to your forehead. Relax your forehead and let any real or imaginary wrinkles go. Now down to your eyes, cheeks, mouth and chin. Let your jaw and whole face relax.

2. Mantra Module

Begin using your mantra as described in "How to use your mantra" above.
After 20 mins when your timer sounds and/or you have reached the end of your meditation move on to the light visualisation exercise below.

3 Light Visualisation Module

This module should only take up a couple of minutes. However, take as long as you need too if you feel anxious or stressed. Sometimes, it is possible that released stress is still awaiting processing at the end of a meditation session.

At the end of your meditation, stop your mantra and visualise a bright round beam of white light mixed with pink and purple heart shapes coming down from the sky/heavens wide enough to surround your whole body.

See your body within this tube of light and see the light moving down into your body from above, through your head and down through your entire body and out through your feet into the Earth below your feet. Notice how this light beam stretches and pulls your feet and legs into the Earth below. See this light continue into the Earth and then back into the sky again, so it forms a complete circle. See your body within this big circle and circuit of white energy. Notice different parts of your body as the light travels down through it. Let your body experience this moving continuous circuit of light and energy. Notice how your body feels.

As you practice, you may notice a warm feeling in your body as if it was becoming energised. However, be open to all possibilities, there are no right or wrong feelings and its OK if you do not get any at all!

Simple summary:

1. Select and practice your mantra
2. Sit upright comfortably in a place where you will not be disturbed for 20 minutes
3. Close your eyes and, focus on your feet then progressively relax your body from your feet to the top of your head.
4. Start your mantra and perhaps, subtly noticing the gaps/space between each repetition
5. When thoughts intrude, gently favour your mantra

EXERCISE 22:

Now write in your Course Journal how you found the above meditation and keep a record of your experiences with this meditation technique.

If you are new to meditation, you will undoubtedly experience a lot of intruding thoughts during your meditation. So, for help with this, now go to the next section and practice the techniques described as you continue to practice your meditation for at least one 20-minute session a day, preferably two sessions a day.

Some of the techniques to control your thoughts in the next section can be used outside of your meditation sessions in the course of your everyday life.

8 Thought and Emotion Control

"Knowing Yourself - The true in the false, gradually strips away all self-delusion until all that remains is pure being." Barry Long

Your internal thought dialogues

Your thoughts and internal dialogue can be helpful in solving life's problems, navigating you through everyday life and working out solutions. However, you will have noticed that often your thoughts runaway out of your control. These thoughts at best are non-productive and often negative. This involves worry, fear about the future, persistently reviewing events and making up future scenarios. Often these thoughts produce a wave of emotion and then the negative thoughts get carried on this wave of negative emotion. This makes an overwhelming combination.

By practicing the Vedic meditation in the previous section, you will start to gain control over your thoughts. However, as you continue with your meditation practice, I need to explain more about intruding thoughts, there is going to be a lot of them as you start to train your mind. Your aim is to stop your internal thought dialogue, to quieten your mind. Your aim is to just observe whatever you are focusing on, whether it is your body, mantra, your breath or a visualisation. Absolutely no thinking about what you are focusing on or analytically thinking about what you are experiencing or doing.

Despite your best efforts you will find your mind running off on a train of thoughts. Then, you will realise what is happening and return back to your meditation. You may be inclined to get frustrated. But please do not! If you do, it will only make your meditation more difficult. Instead, you should know that each time you realise you have run off on a stream of thoughts and stop and return to your meditation, you are gaining more control of your mind. It may be only for short periods to start with but, it will gradually get longer. Anything that can be made to obey for a few seconds can be made to obey forever. When your mind is still without any thoughts, your higher self is the quiet observer.

Each time you notice thoughts intruding, you gain a degree of self-separation. There is the part of you that suddenly realised and noticed the thoughts and stopped them. Like the deep ocean noticing the waves (thoughts) on its surface in my previous analogy of the mind. There are two parts of you, the part that stopped the thoughts is the deep powerful silent part of you.

To help you gain control of intruding thoughts, when you notice that a thought has intruded into your meditation, try this technique: freeze the intruding thought in your mind's eye and then trace your thoughts back by linking and connecting backwards to where the first one intruded into your meditation. Sometimes you get side-tracked and have to start again. But that is how it is as you practice. Another way of describing this technique is by using an analogy of a movie or film. So, for example, when you realise your mind has run off on a train of thoughts, see that train of thoughts as a movie or length of film made up of individual sections or scenes. Each section or scene represents a thought. Each section/thought is logically linked together and runs forward like a movie. This technique is complemented by using a "Pause Button" as explained next.

The Pause Button
When you finally realise you are thinking again whilst you should be meditating, visualise the symbol representing a pause button consisting of two parallel lines, the type found on your remote control that pauses a film. Then place the imaginary pause button over the image of the thought in your mind with the intention of pausing and freezing that thought in its tracks. Effectively leaving you with a still image in your mind, just like you would get if you paused a film on your computer, phone or television screen.

When you have frozen the thought, imagine pressing an imaginary rewind button to review all the previous thoughts linked to it. So, you are effectively rewinding the film of your previous thoughts in your mind backwards reviewing each thought in turn until you get back to where you left your meditation. Then return to your meditation/mantra. Sometimes you may lose your way, but this is a great way for gaining control over your thoughts and getting better at meditating. Practice and persistence are the key.

A powerful variation of the above technique is to pause and freeze your thought by visualising a pause button over it as described above. Then see the frozen thought in three dimensions (3D) and observe it from different angles, notice that it is not part of you, notice that the thought is not real and therefore it is a false part of you, which the real part of you can control. You have just experienced self-separation. Keep practicing!

It is very important not to get annoyed with yourself when you discover a thought intruding. I will say it again! It is very important not to get annoyed with yourself when you discover a thought intruding. If you do, your conscious mind is criticising itself, you feel bad, and it will be detrimental to your meditation. So just observe that you have stopped a train of thoughts again and go back to your meditation. You could visualise the pause button described above and rewind your thoughts as above. Then continue with your meditation. At other times, just stop your thoughts and return to your mantra or visualisation exercise.

EXERCISE 23:
Now go to your Course Journal and complete the exercise on adding thought rewind and the pause button technique to your daily meditation.

Active meditation during your normal day
When you start to practice meditation, you are attempting to train your mind by controlling your thoughts. This means that you are gaining the ability to stop your thinking or train of thoughts should you wish to do so. You are practicing this during meditation because meditation is about quietening your mind. But you can also practice stopping your thoughts during your normal daily activities. This will not only help you become fully proficient at meditation quicker. It will also give you more control over your thoughts in your daily life. This will become invaluable in the future if you find yourself in an emotionally charged state with runaway worrying thoughts. However, even in its normal state of operation, your mind can and does, run off on a train of thoughts you would rather not be thinking. For these reasons you will find the practice of active meditation very valuable, and the good thing is, it won't take up any more of your time!

You will effectively be practicing self-separation because you will be observing from a mentally silent but nevertheless alert state. Notice how an animal (such as your pet) can do this. The part of you that is doing the observing is your higher self. It works at a higher level where thoughts are not required. It is a state of instant knowing. You could compare it to analogue and digital in electrical terms. Thoughts are equivalent to the slow less powerful analogue device and your higher self to the faster and more powerful digital device.

EXERCISES 24 to 28:
Now go to your Journal Workbook and complete the following exercises:

Exercise 24: Adverts
When listening to a commercial radio station, focus on only hearing the words. Suspend all mental dialogue. Do not analyse what is being said. Do not judge what is being said. Have no thoughts. Just hear the sound with your internal dialogue suspended and frozen. Just focus on what is being said. Observe only, listen with a silent mind. No opinions or judgments. Do the same with a visual and audio advert on television for example.

Exercise 25: In conversations
When engaged in conversations, observe your reaction to what is being said. What assumption are you making?

On hearing strangers talking in public places. Observe your curiosity, see yourself getting imaginarily involved in other people's events. Then stop your thoughts and just hear their words. Listen with silence.

Exercise 26: Judgments
When thinking about someone, notice your judgments about that person. Observe yourself making that judgment. It is your false self, making that judgment. Your higher self does not judge.

Exercise 27: Exercise when walking
Observe the movement of your legs and arms, keep your head level and observe your surroundings seeing how it changes as you walk. You could pick just one aspect of your surroundings such as the trees, grass, or pavement. Observe only, no internal dialogue, no thinking, no opinions, no judgements.

Exercise 28: Meditate in idle moments
On the train or bus or in bed for example.

Meditation technique for removing negative feelings & emotions as they arise
This time, instead of observing your body as in a progressive relaxation, you are going to be observing your negative feelings and emotions. This can also be done outside of your usual meditation session in a wide-awake state whenever you can stop your daily activity for five minutes.

This method just involves observing your emotion. In this way the emotion, the false part of you, will dissolve. The false part dies. When the false part dies it is like being a heart broken lover who now discovers they are finally free of feeling for their former lover.

So, when you notice you have a negative emotion or feeling, stop your thoughts and just observe the emotion with no thoughts until the emotion dissolves. Persist just observing until the emotion or negative feeling finally disappears.

So, notice where in your body you have the feeling you want to remove. Focus on it silently, do not think about it, just notice how it feels as you focus on the feeling without analysis and without judgment. Do not think, just feel and observe. You must remain the uninvolved observer so no analysis, no reasoning, do not condemn. Do not try to change anything, just observe. No thinking or internal dialogue.

As you persist in this way, you will notice the bad feeling starts to disappear and then as you continue to persist as I have indicated above, the bad/negative feeling will disappear completely. Make sure you persist until the feeling subsides, it will, but you must persist with no thoughts, just observe.

You are practicing self-separation; your higher self is the observer, and your negative emotion or feeling is the observed. The observed is the false in you, it's not a natural part of you, it wasn't with you when you were born. As the real higher you, observes the false you, the false will get disregarded just as you would disregard anything else you discovered was false in your daily life.

Up until now, you have experienced your negative feelings and simultaneously thought about them whilst you were experiencing them. This has meant you were using the false part of you, the ego/personality that houses those negative feelings to observe itself. That means the negative emotion or feeling stays with you longer and returns often. When you observe your negative or bad feeling in mental silence, it is your true and higher self doing the observing not your ego/personality, so the false gets dissolved, and therefore is less likely to return.

Nobel Prize winner Doctor David R. Hawkins, MD., Ph.D. in his book "Power Versus Force, The Hidden Detriments of Human Behaviour", writes that from an early age he experienced profound deep states of meditation and wrote "… I discovered that I could perceive the reality that underlay personalities; I saw how the origin of emotional sickness lay in people's belief that they were their personalities. And so, of its own, my practice resumed and eventually became huge…".

If the feeling does return it may originate from a different part of you. The important thing is that you keep repeating the meditation process I have described above each time a negative emotion or feeling arises and persist with it. And remember, you can do this exercise in your full daily active waking state outside of your dedicated meditation practice.

To help with the above exercise, you can use and adapt the "Pause Button Technique" I have described earlier in this section. Here it is again: Whilst you are attempting to stop your thoughts and just focus on your feeling or emotion, first visualise the symbol representing a pause button of the type found on your remote control, that pauses a film consisting of two parallel lines. Then place it over the image of the thought in your mind with the intention of pausing and freezing the thought in its tracks. Effectively leaving you with a still image, just like you get if you paused a film on your computer, phone or television screen. This is an effective way of stopping your train of thought, as without movement thoughts will cease and lose their power.

Additionally, to help further, whilst attempting to silently observe your emotion or feeling with no thoughts, you could keep repeating your mantra as you used previously in the Vedic / Altered State Meditation technique in the previous section.

Napoleon Hill said, "Persistence in man is what carbon is to steel". What he meant was, if you persist with something, you can and will achieve whatever you set your mind upon. Your persistence is as strong as carbon cutting through steel.

EXERCISE 29: Meditation technique for removing negative feelings & emotions as they arise

Take the time to memorise and become familiar with the above meditation technique so the next time you experience a negative feeling or emotion you are ready to work to dissolve it. So next time you have a negative emotion or feeling arise use the above technique and record how you got on in your Course Journal.

I will finish this last meditation section with two quotes:

"The purpose of meditation is to transcend the mind and its mental activities and limited perceptions, thereby transcending duality and becoming increasingly aware of Oneness".

Doctor David R. Hawkins, MD., Ph.D.

"In observing your feelings, emotions, habits (the false) your higher self is doing the observing and so is the observer. By being the still detached observer of the observed you are separating yourself out".

Barry Long

EXERCISE 30: Summary of your meditation so far

Now go to your Course Journal and write a summary of your daily meditation progress so far.

Well done for completing this section. Remember to have a meditation session at least once a day and do not forget to practice controlling your thoughts outside of your meditation sessions as described in this section.

Now read the next section on the Spiritual Approach to gain a deeper understanding of meditation.

9 The Spiritual Part

"All I want to do is think like God"
The scientist, Albert Einstein

In the meditation section of this course, I wrote about practicing self-separation. So, your higher self is observing the false part, the negative emotions, or feelings. In meditation self-separation also involves your higher self silently observing other things such as your thoughts, parts of your body and virtually anything else its attention is directed too. You will see that there must be at least two parts of you if one part is observing the other.

One of the aims of meditation is detachment from the notion that your thoughts are you and that is all there is to you. There is much more to you. Consciousness calibration research has shown that ninety-nine percent of the mind is silent. Your thoughts are associated with and influenced by your personality and ego. And so, could be grouped together as your conscious mind and subconscious mind. Leaving the other part of you, your higher self. The great masters going back over three thousand years and beyond, to the Vedic ancient knowledge say that meditation is designed to contact the higher self, the spiritual self, or soul.

So now we have the higher self grouped with the spiritual self, or soul. It is in fact the one and the same. This is the real you I have written about earlier. I am just adding information about it now that we have reached this spiritual section! It is the part of you that never dies, the eternal part of you. To give you an analogy, the ego and personality of a person are like the transient waves on top of an ocean whilst the higher self, spiritual self or soul is like the deep still ocean underneath. However, most people's perception is firmly seated in the waves. So, the person thinks that they are the waves. To put it another way, most people think they are their personality, when in fact they are comprised of so much more. The personality is not eternal, but the higher self is.

What I have written above, is well known ancient spiritual knowledge which you can check out by reading the books listed in the bibliography section of this course. Later, you will see how quantum science and physics supports much of what the spiritual masters have been saying. However, depending on your beliefs, current life history and where you are in the scheme of things, you may find it hard to accept what I have written above. That being the case, which of the two possibilities below makes you feel good?

You are an eternal higher self/spiritual self/soul and so are currently an infinite consciousness having an experience as (insert your name here).

It is just you, flesh and bones and personality, that is all there is. When your dead that is it, you are gone for ever!

I would suggest the first one! So why not at least take it on board as a theory for now, as it will make you feel so much better!

Moving on, this higher self of yours has a connection to an intelligent creative cosmic force to which different cultures throughout history have given different names. These include God, but the definition of "God" has often been slightly distorted by some religions to maintain control over their worshipers.

Carl Jung said, "One of the main functions of organised religion is to protect people against a direct experience of God". So, lets define God as an infinite non personal, non-judgmental and the highest spiritual creative force located on a plane of existence beyond the physical plane. In fact, the physical plane is created from this higher cosmic plane. Before the advent of modern quantum science, it used to be just the spiritual masters claiming this. Now this is confirmed by quantum science / quantum mechanics.

Here is a brief simplified explanation. As we look at matter, we find molecules then atoms, then electrons, then subatomic particles and then sub-subatomic particles. Ultimately, if we were to place these tiny quantum subatomic particles into a particle accelerator and collide them trying to find their source, we would discover what famous scientists such as Albert Einstein and Max Planck discovered.

Max Planck
Max Planck received the Nobel prize in Stockholm Sweden in 1918 for his work on the atom. He was considered to be the greatest scientific mind of his time. Much later in a speech in Florence, Italy in 1944 he made the following speech:
"*As a man who has devoted his whole life to the most clear-headed science, to the study of matter, I can tell you as a result of my research about atoms this much: There is no matter as such. All matter originates and exists only by virtue of a force which brings the particles of an atom to vibration and holds this most minute solar system of the atom together. We must assume behind this force the existence of a conscious and intelligent spirit. This spirit is the matrix of all matter, it is the source of all matter and you listening, you here in this room, all of us are made up of particles that we call matter*"

Another quote by Max Planck:
"*In all my research I have never come across matter. To me the term matter implies a bundle of energy which is given form by an intelligent spirit*".

Albert Einstein
Albert Einstein had come to the same conclusion when he said "*All I want to do is think like God*"

Three further quotes by Albert Einstein:
"*We are slowed down sound and light waves, a walking bundle of frequencies tuned into the cosmos. We are souls dressed up in sacred biochemical garments and our bodies are the instruments through which our souls play their music*".

"*The more I study science, the more I believe in God*".

"*I want to know all Gods thoughts; all the rest are just details*".

David Bohm
The theoretical physicist David Bohm is mostly known for his work in quantum physics. But he also deeply explored the nature of thought and consciousness. Here are four of his quotes relevant to what I am trying to explain here:

"*Ultimately, the entire universe has to be understood as a single undivided whole*".

"*Thought creates our world, and then says, 'I didn't do it*".

"*To change your reality, you have to change your inner thoughts*".

"*We are internally related to everything, not [just] externally related. Consciousness is an internal relationship to the whole, we take in the whole, and we act toward the whole. Whatever we have taken in determines basically what we are. Wholeness is a kind of attitude or approach to the whole of life. If we can have a coherent approach to reality, then reality will respond coherently to us*".

In quantum science, the observer influences the experiment, this has been demonstrated in a number of experiments including the double slit experiment. Therefore, we have eminent quantum scientists and spiritual gurus coming to a consensus that there is a higher (non-personal) spiritual cosmic intelligence often called God behind all creation (including us) and that we are part of that creation and therefore, can influence creation with our own thoughts. Your higher self, the real you, the part that is timeless and eternal is part of this force often called God. And being the higher and real and eternal part of you, has a much stronger connection to "God".

When you enter a thoughtless state in meditation this is called transcendence. You then gain direct connection to your higher self and the higher spiritual force often called "God". You do not need to be an experienced meditator for this to happen, you only need to be in this thoughtless state for seconds to transcend and reap the benefits.

Through continued use of the right type of meditation such as Vedic Meditation as explained in this course, the higher self seems to become more integrated with one's personality. Benefits of this include a much more relaxed outlook on life where the things that used to stress you no longer bother you. You also begin to develop an understanding that we are all ultimately connected to each other. This greatly improves our interactions with other people. There is an old native American proverb that says "No tree has branches so foolish as to fight amongst themselves"

Why am I telling you all this? What did Albert Einstein mean when he said, "All I want to do is think like God." If you understand the laws or the operating system of God / cosmic creative force, work with them and incorporate them into your life, you are going to have an easy time. Just like sitting in a boat flowing with the direction of the river. Working against the way the cosmic creative force works, will mean life will be like trying to paddle against the oncoming water of the river. Better to go with the flow and the force!

An example would be to get creative in a hobby or occupation that really interests you. This cosmic creative force is always creating and therefore you are in the flow. If being creative involves something you are good at and really inspires you, you are inspired … in spirit. As I wrote in an earlier section, this helps greatly with anxiety and mental health problems. Spending time in nature which I also wrote about earlier, helps with mental health problems, as you are closer to God, the creative cosmic force.

If you wish to be in harmony with the power of God, the creative cosmic force and go with the flow for an easier life, in addition to being creative, be kind to yourself and others. A fundamental attribute of the creative cosmic force is kindness. All that is manifested is brought here to thrive, this takes a kindly power. Also, do not judge others, this creative force does not judge. So, if you find yourself judging others you are going against the natural creative flow of life.

So, coming back to meditation. Our aim is to still the mind, to obtain some silence and space between our thoughts. Creation and matter come from space and silence. If you look out of your window and see a tree, it came from a seed, made up of particles such as electrons and subatomic quarks. These came from the void/space/silence as documented by the aforementioned quantum scientists, as the result of a spiritual intelligent force often called God. Saint Paul said "… that which is seen hath not come from what doth appear". What he meant was, matter does not produce matter, it comes from the emptiness, the void, and the silence I have written about in this section, the silence between our thoughts. That is why entering the transcendence state of no thoughts in meditation even if only for a few seconds, is so beneficial on so many levels.

EXERCISE 31:
Now go to your Course Journal to complete the quiz for this section.

10 Hypnotherapy and Hypnosis

"Day by day, in every way, I am getting better and better"

Emile Coue

When working as a hypnotherapist and when first meeting a client, I always ask if they have been hypnotised before. If they have not been to a hypnotist or hypnotherapist before, the answer is usually a firm no! I then go on to explain that in fact they have many times without realising it! All hypnosis is really self-hypnosis, a hypnotist or therapist just guides you through it, with your permission.

In the brief period when you are transitioning from being wide awake to asleep and when you are transitioning from sleep to becoming awake, you have briefly entered and left the hypnotic state.

When you have been meditating you will most likely have entered at least a light hypnotic state.

When you have been driving in your vehicle and had subsequently not remembered a part of your journey, you were in a state of hypnosis! But don't worry, you were actually a safer driver during that time because your subconscious mind, the more powerful part of your mind compared to your conscious mind, took over.

As I have said already, there are two parts to your mind, your subconscious mind and your conscious mind. Your conscious mind makes up about 5% of your mental capacity whilst your subconscious mind makes up the rest at 95%. Your conscious mind, the part you are thinking with right now, can only do one thing well at a time. Try reading a book, watching television, and having a conversation all at the same time, it can't be done! On the other hand, your subconscious mind is looking after all your body's countless biological processes, all running at the same time.

Hypnosis gives a better access to your subconscious mind. Your subconscious mind looks after and protects you, because it's your subconscious mind! Therefore, no hypnotist can make you do anything against your will. A stage hypnotist will only be able to get you to do something if you agree to go along with his or her suggestion. Most people who volunteer to perform with a stage hypnotist are by their nature, an extrovert and so enjoy making a show of themselves.

If you have been practicing the Vedic type meditation as taught in this course, you will have entered a light hypnotic state on many occasions as you entered the Alpha state of consciousness.

We can determine your brains frequency by hooking it up to a brain frequency monitor of the type found in a hospital. Different frequencies are associated with different levels of consciousness.

The wide-awake Beta state gives a brain frequency of 12 to 38 cycles per second (hertz).

The Alpha state in which we are very relaxed and possibly daydreaming, gives a brain frequency of between 8 to 12 cycles per second.

The Theta state in which you will be in a deep meditative state has a brain frequency of 3 to 8 cycles per second.

The Delta state has a brain frequency of 0.5 to 3 cycles per second and is a dreamless state.

When you are under hypnosis, you are most likely to be in the Alpha state above. However, in the hypnotic state your senses are heightened, and you are more aware. So, you are certainly not asleep, you are in fact in a heightened state of awareness. For example, if I was sitting next to you and you were experiencing hypnosis and I was wide awake, if the wiring caught fire outside the room in the corridor you would detect the burning smell before I did, because your senses are heightened.

For most people however, the hypnotic process is rather ordinary and non-magical. So, after a hypnotherapy session they may say "it didn't really work for them", they had not gone under and the whole process seemed rather ordinary. But then again, there is no such thing as a hypnotised feeling! So how would they really know? An experienced hypnotherapist would be able to spot physical signs that the client had entered hypnosis.

Therapy whilst in hypnosis is called hypnotherapy, it is predominantly used for two different types of treatments. Suggestion therapy and analytical therapy.

Most people who consult me are either doing something they don't want to do or not doing something they want to do. They would normally expect me to hypnotise them out of it or plant an idea in their mind to change their behaviour etc. While they were in hypnosis, we could indeed plant suggestions in their mind to change their behaviour, to give up smoking or lose weight for example. Suggestion therapy is very effective in helping people give up smoking.

Many people have phobias, an irrational fear of something. For example, heights, water, blood, spiders, mice, flying and small spaces or large spaces. Referred to as claustrophobia and agoraphobia. If you went to a hypnotherapist to try and get rid of your phobia, he or she may indeed go ahead and plant suggestions in your mind to hypnotise you out of it. So, if you were for example, previously afraid of small spaces such as lifts, you may well go away able to get in lifts with no problem at all.

However, if you had come to see me or any other therapist who practices as I do, that's not the sort of therapy I would normally give you. I would not simply plant suggestions in your mind to try and cure your claustrophobia. Why? The person who had been cured of claustrophobia may now find they can't go outside, they are now afraid of large spaces, agoraphobia. What has taken place is symptom substitution. The person as swapped their claustrophobia for agoraphobia.

I would rather avoid the risks of symptom substitution. As I said before, the phobia is an irrational fear inside a person but outside their control. I would rather use a process of recall under hypnosis to look for the actual cause of the problem. Most people think they know what the cause of their problem is. But the truth is if they really did know they wouldn't have the problem. We look at the problem that is in the subconscious part of the mind.

Suggestion therapy still has a role to play and can be used very effectively for such things as smoking, weight loss, to improve sports performance, help with exams and studying etc. However, the type of analytical therapy I use is the best way to deal with irrational fears and phobias, anxiety, and other psychological and emotional problems.

History and Background of Hypnosis and Hypnotherapy

At the risk of putting you into a deep trance here is a little history! Here is a short, action-packed account, picking out the people who have made significant contributions to the development of our understanding of hypnosis.

The earliest references to hypnosis date back to ancient Egypt and Greece. Indeed, Hypnos' is the Greek word for sleep, although the actual state of hypnosis is very different from that of sleep. Both cultures had religious centres where people came for help with their problems. Hypnosis was used to induce dreams, which were then analysed to get to the root of the trouble.

There are many references to trance and hypnosis in early writings. In 2600 BC the father of Chinese medicine, Wong Tai, wrote about techniques that involved incantations and passes of the hands. The Hindu Vedas written around 1500 BC mention hypnotic procedures. Trance-like states occur in many shamanistic, druidic, voodoo, yogic and religions.

HYPNOTIC PIONEERS

The modern father of hypnosis was an Austrian physician, Franz Mesmer (1734 to 1815), from whose name the word 'mesmerise' is derived. Though much maligned by the medical world of his day, Mesmer was nevertheless a brilliant man. He developed the theory of animal magnetism the idea that diseases are the result of blockages in the flow of magnetic forces in the body. He believed he could store his animal magnetism in baths of iron filings and transfer it to patients with rods or by "mesmeric passes".

The mesmeric pass must surely go down in history as one of the most interesting, and undoubtedly the most long-winded, ways of putting someone into a trance. Mesmer would stand his subjects quite still while he swept his arms across their body, sometimes for hours on end. I suspect that this probably had the effect of boring patients into a trance, but it was certainly quite effective. Mesmer himself was very much a showman, conveying by his manner that something was going to happen to the patient. This form of indirect suggestion was very powerful. Mesmer was also responsible for the popular image of the hypnotist as a man with magnetic eyes, a cape and goatee beard.

His success fuelled jealousy among many of his colleagues and this eventually led to his public humiliation. Looking back, it is quite incredible that hypnosis survived these early years, because the medical world was so dead set against it. Another forward thinker was John Elliotson (1791 to 1868), a professor at London University, who is famous for introducing the stethoscope into England. He also tried to champion the cause of mesmerism but was forced to resign. He continued to give demonstrations of mesmerism in his own home to any interested parties, and this led to a steady increase in literature on the subject.

The next real pioneer of hypnosis in Britain appeared in the mid-nineteenth century with James Braid (1795 to1860). Primarily a Scottish eye doctor, he developed an interest in mesmerism quite by chance. One day, when he was late for an appointment, he found his patient in the waiting room staring into an old lamp, his eyes glazed. Fascinated, Braid gave the patient some commands, telling him to close his eyes and go to sleep. The patient complied and Braid's interest grew. He discovered that getting a patient to fixate upon something was one of the most important components of putting them into a trance. The swinging watch, which many people associate with hypnosis, was popular in the early days as an object of fixation. Following his discovery that it was not necessary to go through all the palaver of mesmeric passes, Braid published a book in which he proposed that the phenomenon now be called hypnotism.

Meanwhile, a British surgeon in India, James Esdaile (1808 to 1859), recognised the enormous benefits of hypnotism for pain relief and performed hundreds of major operations using hypnosis as the only anaesthetic. When he returned to England, he tried to convince the medical establishment of his findings, but they laughed at him and declared that pain was character-building. Although they were biased in favour of the new chemical anaesthetics, which they could control and of course, charge more money for. So, hypnosis became and remains to this day, an 'alternative' form of medicine.

The French were also taking an interest in the subject of hypnosis, and many breakthroughs were made by such men as Ambrose Liebeault (1823 to 1904), J. M. Charcot (1825 to 1893) and Charles Richet (1850 to1935). The work of another Frenchman, Emile Coue (1857 to 1926), was very interesting. He moved away from conventional approaches and pioneered the use of auto-suggestion. He is most famous for the phrase, 'Day by day in every way I am getting better and better". His technique was one of affirmation and it has been championed in countless modern books. A man of enormous compassion, Coue believed that he did not heal people himself but merely facilitated their own self-healing. He understood the importance of the subject's participation in hypnosis and was a forerunner of those modern practitioners who claim, 'There is no such thing as hypnosis, only self-hypnosis.

Perhaps his most famous idea was that the imagination is always more powerful than the will. For example, if you ask someone to walk across a plank of wood on the floor, they can usually do it without wobbling. However, if you tell them to close their eyes and imagine the plank is suspended between two buildings hundreds of feet above the ground, they will start to sway.

In a sense Coue also anticipated the placebo effect treatment of no intrinsic value. The power of which lies in suggestion when patients are told they are being given a drug that will cure them. Recent research on placebos is quite startling. In some cases, statistics indicate that placebos can work better than many of modern medicine's most popular drugs. It seems that while drugs are not always necessary for recovery from illness, belief in recovery is!

Sigmund Freud (1856 to 1939) was also interested in hypnosis, initially using it extensively in his work. He eventually abandoned the practice for several reasons. Not least that he probably wasn't any good at it! He favoured psychoanalysis, which involves the patient lying on a couch and the analyst doing a lot of listening. He believed repressed memories of traumatic incidents were the main cause of psychological problems. Freud's early rejection of hypnosis delayed the development of hypnotherapy, turning the focus of psychology away from hypnosis and towards psychoanalysis. However, things picked up in the 1930's in America with the publication of Qark Hull's book, Hypnosis and Suggestibility.

In more recent times, the recognised leading authority on clinical hypnosis was Milton H. Erickson, MD (1901 to 1980), a remarkable man and a highly effective psychotherapist. As a teenager he was stricken with polio and paralysed, but he remobilised himself. It was while paralysed that he had an unusual opportunity to observe people, and he noticed that what people said and what they did were often very different. He became fascinated by human psychology and devised countless innovative and creative ways to help people. He healed through metaphor, surprise, confusion and humour, as well as hypnosis. A master of 'indirect hypnosis', he was able to put a person into a trance without even mentioning the word hypnosis. It is becoming more and more accepted that an understanding of hypnosis is essential for the efficient practice of every type of psychotherapy.

Over the years hypnosis has gained ground and respectability within the medical profession. Although hypnosis and medicine are not the same, they are now acknowledged as being related, and it is only a matter of time before hypnosis becomes a mainstream practice, as acceptable to the general public as a visit to the dentist.

In 1993 the New Scientist magazine published a study which was the largest study ever undertaken into research on stopping smoking methods. The study spanned several continents and finally the New Scientist came up with the verdict that hypnosis is proven to work. Indeed, hypnosis was found to be ahead of anything else on the market when it came to helping people stop smoking. The New Scientist's verdict was that "Hypnosis is as natural as time itself and a gift to us all, once we know of its existence".

I have run through the main pioneers in the exploration and study of hypnosis, and hypnotherapy. But it is also interesting that many creative individuals have used a trance-like state to access their talents. Artists, writers, poets and composers have induced a form of hypnotic trance to help them with their work. The poet Alfred Lord Tennyson (1809 to 1892) would repeat his own name to himself again and again like a mantra, and by doing this would access a different state of consciousness in which whole poems came to him that he could then transcribe. Mozart (1756 to 1791) apparently composed Cosi-fan-Tutte, one of his most famous operas, whilst hypnotised, and Rachmaninov (1873 to 1943) reportedly composed one of his concertos following a post-hypnotic suggestion.

When the University of Strasbourg gave classes in hypnosis, students included the poet and playwright Goethe (1749 to 1832) as well as Thomas Edison (1847 to 1931), Nikola Tesla (1856 to 1943), Henry Ford (1863 to 1947), Albert Einstein (1879 to 1955) and Aldous Huxley (1894 to 1963). All used trance-like states to help in the development of their ideas. Many of history's greatest innovators made documented use of some special level of consciousness. These days, huge numbers of leading athletes, business people and artists in many different fields use similar approaches with great success. The Dalai Lama recently questioned our reasons for sending investigative teams into outer space and under the sea when the real undiscovered treasures of humanity lie within the realms of our minds, and I must say I have to agree with him!

EXERCISE 32:
Now go to your Course Journal to complete the quiz for this section.

EXERCISE 33:
Now go to your Course Journal and complete **the self-hypnosis instruction audio exercise**.

If you need help memorising your self-hypnosis session for use later without the audio, I have printed it below:

Self-Hypnosis procedure

This is similar to the relaxation module from the altered state meditation which you have been practicing. I have reprinted it below. You need to be able to sit or lie down somewhere comfortable where you will not be disturbed for 35 minutes. You can set a timer that is not too startling if you have commitments immediately after your session. Before you start, it is advisable to spend a small amount of time to slowdown and give yourself a bit of space between your daily activities and relax.

Now follow the following progressive relaxation sequence. It is easy to remember and practice. Simply start at the top of your body and slowly work down. Just tense and relax each part in sequence from head to toe. It should take approximately five minutes.

1. Sit upright on your chair or lie down on a sofa or bed.
2. Look upward slightly and fix your eyes on a spot either real or imaginary in front of you.
3. Tell yourself you are going to silently count from 1 to 3 and on the count of 3, your eyes will close, and you will be under hypnosis.
4. Now count slowly from 1 to 3 and let your eyes close on the count of 3.

5. Start your relaxation by fixing your attention on your feet. Begin with your toes, curl your toes, and let them go, notice the sensation as they relax. Let the relaxation rise up into both of your feet. Notice the sensation in your feet.

6. Tense and relax your legs below your knees. Then allow the relaxation to flow up into your calf muscles. Take your time to sense the feeling in your calf muscles.

7. Let the relaxation rise up over your thighs and let both of your legs relax.

8. Now fix your attention on your stomach, relax every muscle, every nerve and every fibre in your stomach as your stomach rests.

9. Now focus on your chest, notice how each deep breath is relaxing you more and more.

10. Now place your attention on your hands and your arms. Begin with your fingers, tightly close your fingers, pause, then open them and feel your hands, relax. Let that relaxation rise up through your hands, wrists, forearms and upper arms. Take your time, notice the physical sensations as your hands, wrists, forearms and upper arms progressively relax.

11. Let that relaxation sweep across your shoulders, notice any areas of tension or tightness in your shoulders, and let it go.

12. Let the relaxation rise up the back of your head, across the top of your head and down to your forehead. Relax your forehead and let any real or imaginary wrinkles go. Now down to your eyes, cheeks, mouth and chin. Let your jaw and whole face relax.

When you have completed the above 12 steps:

Allow yourself to Imagine standing at the top of a flight of steps or stairs, tell yourself that each step is numbered from 1 to 10. Now tell yourself that each step you take down will take you down to deeper levels of relaxation. And when you get to the bottom you will be as relaxed as you can ever be. Now count slowly from 1 to 10 telling yourself you're relaxing further and further with each step you take.

11 Memory & Emotion Recall Therapy

"The conscious mind may be compared to a fountain playing in the sun and falling back into the great subterranean pool of subconscious from which it rises"

Sigmund Freud

Before reading this section, re-read the Initial Consultation Section to refresh your memory.

You will be using your Course Journal in this section.

This section involves detailed work with your memory. Emotions get locked into some memories, normally the painful ones. Often these memories can then become difficult to retrieve and so the emotions stay locked away causing problems. This process was described in detail in the Initial Consultation Section. I will just explain it in a slightly different way here. This was known in ancient times. The AD 10th-12th Century Toltecs in what is now Mexico had a therapy using memory retrieval which they called Recapitulation. It was basically a technique to retrieve and review memories. Which in turn released repressed and hidden feelings and emotions which were causing the types of negative symptoms that I have described in the Initial Consultation Section. Anthropologists such as Carlos Castaneda and Victor Sanchez have documented these recapitulation techniques.

The function of recapitulation according to the ancient Toltec civilisation is summed up beautifully by anthropologist Victor Sanchez.

"Recapitulation is the natural process of energetic restoration of our energetic body from the damages that come from the past. This natural act is done by the body. It consists of bodily remembering and reliving the meaningful events in our lives in order to perform a healing process to recover the state of energetic completeness that we had when we were born".

More recently, Freud used a similar concept in his psychoanalysis methods. However, for the best results it is best to use memory recall with a slight change in one's level of consciousness. Different states of consciousness are associated with different brain frequencies.

As I explained in the Hypnosis and Hypnotherapy section, we can determine your brains frequency by hooking it up to a brain frequency monitor of the type found in a hospital. Different frequencies are associated with different levels of consciousness.

The wide-awake Beta state gives a brain frequency of 12 to 38 cycles per second (hertz).

The Alpha state in which we are very relaxed and possibly daydreaming, gives a brain frequency of between 8 to 12 cycles per second.

The Theta state on which you will be in a deep meditative state has a brain frequency of 3 to 8 cycles per second.

The Delta state has a brain frequency of 0.5 to 3 cycles per second and is a dreamless state.

It has been found that a relaxed state of consciousness associated with the Alpha state (such as that experienced in hypnosis and used in hypnotherapy) considerably helps with memory recall therapy of the type associated with the ancient recapitulation method and the more recent psychoanalysis therapies. For more about hypnotherapy and hypnosis see the previous hypnotherapy and hypnosis section.

This section runs alongside your regular daily meditation program and uses your Course Journal and a one hour a week dedicated self-hypnosis/meditation type session. There are two parts to it, journal work and the dedicated self-hypnosis meditation type session. Just doing the journal part without the dedicated 1-hour altered state meditation/hypnotherapy type session would still give you benefits but the two parts together are considerably more effective. You will however need to persevere. Once you start however, the healing and memory recall process takes on a life of its own. It's like starting a ball rolling down a hill, the healing and memory recall process keeps going between sessions.

Because the process involves retrieving memories from the past, you may sometimes also notice emotions accompanying those memories, all manner of different emotions and feelings, this naturally means that some will be unpleasant. But that's good because those negative feelings and emotions were producing negative symptoms! And when those negative emotions are released, it is like letting a mad rabid dog out of a cage, there is no way you can get it back in again! That particular negative emotion is gone for good.

You start the Journal part first because it provides a start and basis for the 1-hour altered state meditation type session. This is a substitute for an analytical hypnotherapy session normally used face to face with a hypnotherapist. It is based on the free association technique pioneered by Freud but enhanced by the altered alpha conscious state which in this context could be called self-hypnosis. This technique was used extensively by the International Association of Hypnotherapists (IAH) started in the 1970's by Neil French. I was a member of this Association and at one time had three separate clinics helping numerous patients with this method.

Ideally, a one-to-one consultation with a qualified therapist works best with one session a week usually a minimum of eight weeks, frequently many more depending on the severity of the symptoms and how responsive the patient is. This however is dependent on finding a therapist and being able to afford the ongoing session fee, which can be prohibitive if multiple weekly sessions are required. This is what happened to me back in 1985. After a very traumatic childhood, I suffered from anxiety and depression that made it very difficult to talk and interact with people. I had researched and learnt self-hypnosis from books and by luck, living in remote Wales, I managed to find a hypnotherapist specialising in analytical hypnotherapy. I had two sessions which helped immensely in releasing painful emotions. However, it was clear that I would need more sessions.

The only problem was that there was no way I could afford to pay for anymore. I was young and on a low wage at that time. Luckily, I managed to purchase a book published in 1984 by Neil French called "Successful Hypnotherapy, An Investigation of Mankind Under the Microscope of Hypnosis". This gave more details on the analytical free association method. This involved weekly sessions with a suitably qualified therapist. Back to square one, I could not afford to see a suitably qualified therapist!

They say necessity is the mother of all invention. Well, I adapted the free association analysis technique using self-hypnosis, a similar if not the same state experienced in some meditations. I found that anxiety and tension was released in almost all of my sessions. I gave myself two sessions a week and 6 months later, I was feeling considerably better and able to interact and talk with people due to a lack of anxiety. Many years later I went on to train with the IAH and Neil French and qualified in 1998. Subsequently, I have taken many patients successfully through the process. Which at one time involved working from 3 separate clinics.

If I were to put it into my own words to illustrate the goal of this section/module, I would say that my aim would be to get you back to the state that you were in before fate intervened. So, let us get started.

Stage one is journal work where basically; you write down a list summarising with just a heading, your life history in a structured manner. This has three purposes:

1. To serve as a starting point for each therapy session if needed and to provide a structure for therapy if needed. This includes sessions with a therapist if you wish.
2. To help recover hidden memories and their linked associated emotions
3. To function as a practical therapeutic journaling tool in its own right.

So, let us get started with this section of your journal. I recommend putting time aside to write your list in your journal. Ideally an hour each time. Also, work at your list regularly to avoid losing the momentum of recall from the previous session.

EXERCISE 34:
Now go to your Course Journal and start work on part one of your Course Journal work.

EXERCISE 35:
After you have completed Exercise 34 above, go to your Course Journal and start work on part two of your Course Journal work.

Therapy sessions using self-hypnosis
When you have finished or have listed a reasonable number of memories in your Course Journal, you can move on to your 1-hour altered state meditation type session. Let us call them your analytical therapy sessions where you will be using the self-hypnosis technique you practised in Exercise 33. If you have not completed Exercise 33 go back and complete it now, before proceeding any further.

Your analytical therapy sessions work in a similar way to your meditation sessions but last longer. Usually, up to an hour. There are three separate parts to the session.

1. Relaxation module using the self-hypnosis technique in Exercise 33
2. Free association exercise
3. Session closing procedure

Free Association Module
Free association works by linking one memory to another without judgment or analytical thought. One memory just links to another memory just like parts of a conversation naturally flow from one topic to another. I will explain further by using an analogy. Imagine a large, long chain made up of its separate links. Each separate link

represents a memory. As you get to one link it automatically leads to another. If you look down the length of the long chain, you will see all memories are ultimately linked to each other. This is the same within your subconscious mind. Some of those memories will be hidden down the chain, some of these hidden memories will have painful emotions attached which will be causing negative symptoms. By recalling the memories before this problematic memory, you will get to the one causing the problem and automatically release the emotion attached to it which was having a negative effect on you.

It is absolutely vital that you don't analyse what you are remembering, you just want a running commentary of the recollection or memory. This is the right way for example:

"I am riding down the street on my bike and I am getting wet because it's raining".

The following is intellectualising and not what we want:

"I am riding down the street on my bike and I am getting wet because it is raining. Now when did I get that bike? I wonder which birthday it was.

So, we just want a running commentary of your memory. Unless you are with your therapist there is no need to speak out aloud.

You can start the session using a memory from your journal if one does not arise. Likewise, you can take another memory from your journal if your memories come to a halt during the session. So, I would suggest taking time to quickly review your journal before starting the free association module, so you do not need to refer to it during the free association part of your session.

If any painful memories arise take some slow deep breaths until the feeling goes. You can also use the Emo-Trance method from the Fast Guide Section to release any tensions or bad feelings as they arise. So, make sure you practice this beforehand, and that you understand the procedure. You can also cut a session short if you are struggling with bad feelings and spend 20 mins in meditation to calm down and relax.

Whilst retrieving and reliving your memories, see if you can remember if there were any smells or aromas that came to you at that time. Also, if you felt or touched something, what did it feel like and what texture did it have? What emotions associated with that memory did you experience? What were you doing with your body? Were you sitting, walking, standing, or moving your hands for example? What could you see? What could you hear? And was there any speech or talking present? Proceed in this order if you can.

Closing the session

When your hour is up, and your timer sounds or before that if you have had enough, it is time to close the session. Sometimes you may just feel that it is enough, so then it is OK to stop. When I was doing it on my own, I would feel that my head was full and just knew it was time to end the session. Anyway, when you are ready to end the session, I would suggest taking a few deep breaths and just letting your mind drift to a peaceful place and relax there for a few minutes. Then tell yourself that you are going to count backwards from 3 to 1 and that on the count of 1 you will open your eyes and be wide awake.

EXERCISE 36:

Now go to your Course Journal and start work on your first analytical therapy session.

EXERCISE 37:

After you have completed exercise 36 above, repeat exercise 36 at least once a week or every three days if you feel able to, and it suits you. Keep a record of your progress in Exercise 37. If you are working with a therapist, one session a week is usually recommended.

EXERCISE 38:

When you have completed all the exercises and feel that your presenting symptoms previously listed in Exercise 1, Your Initial Consultation, have reduced or been eliminated, please go to your Course Journal and complete your progression plan.

Finally, now at the end of this course, I will leave you with two considerations and would suggest that you remember them always, wherever you are and whatever you find yourself experiencing:

You are a powerful infinite eternal consciousness currently having an experience as …. (insert your name here).

"We tend to forget that happiness doesn't come as a result of getting something we don't have, but rather recognising and appreciating what we do have". Frederick Koenig

EXERCISE 39: Course Evaluation

I hope you have benefited from this course. Your feedback is important so I can continue to improve the course in the future to help others. Therefore, if you would like to go to your Course Journal for the last time to complete the course evaluation form, that would be greatly appreciated.

Bibliography

Successful Hypnotherapy by Neil French

Introductory Lectures on Psychoanalysis Lecture 24, The Common Neurotic State by Sigmund Freud

Introductory Lectures on Psychoanalysis by Sigmund Freud

The Toltec Path of Recapitulation by Victor Sanchez

Science of Being and Art of Living, Transcendental Meditation by Maharishi Mahesh Yogi

The Power of Intention by Dr Wayne Dyer

Oceans of Energy, The Patterns & Techniques of Emo-Trance, Volume 1 by Doctor Silvia Hartmann

About the Author

Paul Craddock is the author of four books including Therapy for Your Mind. He has had a lifelong interest in alternative therapies specialising in psychotherapy, hypnotherapy, self-development and more recently in meditation techniques. He is constantly researching, experimenting and successful using and applying new therapeutic techniques in the above fields. He is a qualified hypnotherapist and psychotherapist previously operating from 3 different clinics.

COURSE JOURNAL

For use with The Anxiety Therapy Workbook

By Paul Craddock DHP

To download and print a hard copy go to **www.anxietytherapy.info**

WRITE YOUR NAME BELOW:

....

Disclaimer

This Journal is intended to complement and support, not replace normal allopathic medicine or medical treatment. If you suffer from any acute or chronic disease you should always seek medical attention from a qualified doctor immediately. The author and publisher accept no liability or damage of any nature resulting directly or indirectly from the application or use of any information contained within this Journal.

The author and publisher of this Journal and the accompanying materials have used their best efforts in preparing this Journal. The author and publisher make no representation or warranties with respect to the accuracy, applicability, fitness or completeness of the contents of this Journal. The information contained in this Journal is strictly for educational purposes. Therefore, if you wish to apply ideas and techniques contained in this Journal, you are taking full responsibility for your actions.

Exercise 1 (Section 3):
Personal Details & Initial Consultation Form

CONFIDENTIAL

Name:

Age:

Date you enrolled on this course:

Address or location:

Email:

Phone number:

Preferred method of contact:

Occupation:

WHAT ARE YOUR PRESENTING SYMPTOMS?

List and describe your symptoms and state how long you have had them. This would typically be referred to as something inside of you but out of your control such as depression, anxiety, phobias, excess stress, panic attacks.

SEVERITY

With regard to severity, (how bad the symptoms/s are) give them a number from 1 to 10 with 1 having the least effect and 10 the most extreme or worse effect.

Do you suffer from excess stress at work? If yes, please give details:

Is a personal relationship causing you stress? If yes, please give details:

Do you want to lose weight or to stop smoking/vaping? If you need to stop smoking/vaping what is the frequency of your current habit? If you need to lose weight how much do you need to lose?

Details of previous or ongoing therapy or treatment:

Personal details and Initial Consultation Form continued:

Other information:

Exercise 2 (Section 3):
Stress Test

Please tick the box that applies to you. Answer yes, even if only part of a question applies to you. Take your time, but please be totally honest with your answers.

		Yes	No
1	I frequently work at home at night, on work which I have brought home		
2	I feel that there are just not enough hours in the working day to do all of the things that I must do		
3	I can frequently feel impatient with the speed at which events take place		
4	At times I can have an extreme reluctance to go to work		
5	I try to fit more and more tasks into less and less time, resulting in me not allowing time for any unforeseen problems that may arise		
6	I feel that there are too many deadlines in my work / life that are difficult to meet		
7	My self-confidence / self-esteem is low		
8	I can frequently have a vaguely guilty feeling if I relax and do nothing, even for short periods of time		
9	I find myself thinking about problems to do with my personal / business/professional life, even when I am supposed to be engaged in recreational pursuits		
10	I can have a feeling of intense fatigue, even when I wake after sleep		
11	I can / do find myself finishing other people's sentences for them		
12	I have a tendency to eat, talk, move and walk quickly		

13	My appetite has altered, to a desire to go on a binge, especially on sweet, sugary foods. Or, I have suffered a loss of appetite		
14	I find myself becoming irritated / angry if the car or traffic in front of me seems to me to be going too slowly / I become very frustrated at having to wait in a queue		
15	I can feel anger and resentment at nothing in particular and or, a feeling that something is missing, but I don't know what		
16	I'm aware that I try to get other people to hurry up / get on with it		
17	At times I feel depressed, tearful, irritable, all-over tension, short tempered, unusual clumsiness, my concentration / memory is impaired.		
18	I find that if I have to do repetitive tasks, I become impatient		
19	I can seem to be listening to other people's conversations, even though I am in fact preoccupied with my own thoughts		
20	I find myself grinding my teeth, especially if I am stressed or feeling impatient		
21	I seem to have an increase in aches and pains, especially in the neck, head, jaw, lower back, shoulders, and chest. For women: Menstrual cycles are erratic, often missed		
22	At times I am unable to perform work or tasks as well as I used too, or I feel my judgment is clouded / not as good as it was		
23	I find I have a greater dependency on alcohol, caffeine, nicotine or drugs (whether prescription or not)		
24	I find that I don't have time for many interests / hobbies outside of work		

A yes answer scores 1 (one), and a no answer scores 0 (zero).

Now, total up all of your yes scores: ………………………………..

If you score:

4 points or less: You have no need to worry about being prone to stress. You are least likely to suffer from stress-related illness.

5 - 13 points: You are prone to stress. You are also more likely to suffer from the negative effects of stress. Long term, you may possibly be open to stress-related illness. I would recommend that you start working through this course as you are in need of stress control management / counselling.

14 points or more: You are the most prone to the negative effects of stress. And so, you are more open to serious stress-related illness. I would recommend that you start working through this course making sure you stay on the long-term therapies that we cover in this course. It may also be worth considering the premium version of this course for ongoing tutor support.

Exercise 3 (Section 4):
Setting up your Personal Journal

As explained in this section, obtain a physical journal/notebook or set up your digital journal to use as your personal journal. Your Personal Journal will run alongside this Course and Workbook Journal. You will be able to share information from your Personal Journal with your tutor through your Course Journal and workbook should you choose that option.

Personal Journal Sections
Apart from your general observations which you could record in a daily diary format, it can be useful to divide your journal into sections or headers.

Daily diary

Therapy journal (to record your therapy)

Specific problems & projects

Personal development, goals and plans

Gratitude journal

Business journal

However, to start with, just use your Personal Journal daily to record your progress, thoughts and experiences as you work through this Course Journal. However, whether you have made an entry in your Course Journal or not, use your Personal Journal daily as instructed in the Course Journal section. Note: For the first 30 days you may find it helpful to tick off each day on a calendar so you can see you are maintaining and being consistent with your journal entries.

You may also find it very helpful to start your gratitude section daily if you skip ahead and read "expressing gratitude" in Section 5. Just write what you are grateful for every day you use your Personal Journal. Record your progress:

Date you set up your Personal Journal:

For the next 30 days write down the date and time you make an entry in your Personal Journal:

For the next 30 days write down the date and time you make an entry in your Personal Journal. Continued:

Exercise 4 (Section 5):

Guided meditation, relaxation and hypnotherapy audio

Go to the Resource Appendix at the end of this journal and access the guided meditation/relaxation/hypnotherapy audio.

Listen to the guided meditation/relaxation/hypnotherapy audio as instructed in this section. I would suggest daily or every other day. At bedtime just before you go to sleep is good. The suggestions will still work even if you fall asleep.

Record your results below for the next 30 days:

The dates you used the recording and your experience each time:

Exercise 4 continued. Experiences with guided meditation, relaxation and hypnotherapy audio:

Exercise 5 (Section 5):
The Pause Button

Practice the pause button procedure on your unwanted thoughts as they travel through your mind. When you place the pause button over your thought, see the thought frozen in front of you like a clip of film. Practice this at least 12 times and record your results below with the date:

Exercise 5 the pause button continued:

Exercise 6 (Section 5):
The "I am responsible" affirmation

When you are having a negative thought repeat the "I am responsible" affirmation at least 3 times in sequence. Record your response with dates below:

Exercise 7 (Section 5):

The fan procedure

Practice the fan procedure on your unwanted thoughts as they travel through your mind. Make a note of your results. Which method for stopping your thoughts works best for you?

Exercise 8: (Section 5)
Walk in nature:

Write down when and where you can go for a short walk in nature if only for 20 minutes around the park or similar.

How did you feel afterwards?

Now make a plan as to how you can make this a regular occurrence:

Exercise 9 (Section 5): Get in Spirit and Inspired:

Write down what you will do:

Exercise 10 (Section 5): The Calm Technique:

(1) Practice the Calm Technique now in preparation for when you need to use it and record your results below:

(2) Use it when you need immediate help and make a note of the result:

Exercise 11 (Section 5): The Emo-Trance Technique:

Memorise the summary below and write it down to check you have memorised it correctly.

Locate and identify the specific area in your body where you are feeling the negative symptom, painful feeling or emotion. Observe its boundaries and see it as a defined mass of solid energy which is producing the feeling you are experiencing.

Now, without thinking about the likely answer, ask yourself what colour the feeling/mass of energy is?

Now see it as a solid colour.

Now imagine breathing into this solid colour and see your breath breaking up this defined area. As it breaks up, see it disintegrating into grains of sand or vapour in the colour you gave it.

Now as this solid area breaks up into grains of sand or vapour, notice which way it is moving to exit through your body from its defined area. Do not think about it, just notice which way it is moving out through your body. Notice which path it takes as it exits your body. There is no right or wrong way.

Keep breathing into the defined area whilst observing it breaking up into grains of sand or vapour and moving out through your body in its preferred direction until the feeling completely disappears.

Next time you have a negative feeling use the above Emo-Trance technique and make a note of how you got on in this exercise:

Exercise 11 Emo Trance:

Exercise 12 (Section 5): Externalisation and Identification:

What can you divert your focus on to feel better?

Exercise 13 (Section 5): Depression

If you are suffering from depression, what small thing will you do right now?

Exercise 14 (Section 5) Physical Exercise

What exercise would work for you to relieve stress?

Make a plan or schedule to enable you to complete this exercise. Remember it only needs to be for 10 minutes a day. Write your plan or schedule down below:

Exercise 15 (Section 5):
How to stop worrying

(1 Write down what is the exact cause of your worry:

(2) Write down all the possible scenarios and possibilities:

(3) Write down the worst-case scenario, what is the worst that could happen?

(4) Now accept the worst-case scenario in your mind, just for a few moments.

(5) Now write down a list of things you can do to avoid the worst-case scenario:

Exercise 16 (Section 5):
Expressing gratitude:

Every night before you go to bed, write down 3 good things that has happened to you that you can be grateful for. You may want to observe what they might be throughout the day.

Alternatively, when you awake in the morning, think of one thing you are grateful for. You may want to place a small pebble or crystal or small keepsake object in your pocket to make yourself remember what you are grateful for each time you feel the object in your pocket throughout the day. People have called this their "gratitude stone".

Record what you are grateful for every day for the next 30 days in this Course Journal below. After 30 days switch to recording your gratitude in your Personal Journal ongoing.

Exercise 16 Expressing Gratitude:

Exercise 17 (Section 5):
Don't take yourself too seriously!

Next time you find yourself getting impatient, remember the story with the above name in this section and tell yourself to stop taking yourself so seriously. Make a note of the occasions below:

Exercise 18 (Section 5): Paradoxical Intention

1. First you need to identify and quantify the symptom you are experiencing that you want relief from. You may find it helpful to consider the following:

Are you not doing something that you want to do?

Are you doing something that you don't want to do?

Are you getting anxious about being anxious?

Which thoughts cause you anxiety?

What are you afraid of?

What situation are you afraid of?

What or who causes you anxiety?

Where in your body do feel the anxiety?

2. So now write down what is the event or situation that will make you anxious?

3. Now write how in your imagination you can exaggerate your fear to the extent that it becomes humorous and ridiculous.

4. Now put this into practice and keep a record of how you got on below:

Exercise 19 (Section 6):
Quiz: Introduction to meditation

(1) What are the two stages of meditation?

Multiple choice: select the correct ones:

Concentration

Sleep

Mindfulness

Dreaming

Thoughtless awareness

(2) Name 5 observed benefits of meditation

Multiple choice: select the correct ones:

Help with mental health problems

You become more friendly

Lower blood pressure

You will become a vegetarian

Reduced stress levels

Help with sleep

Increase your appetite

Help with Post-traumatic stress disorder

Help with Addictions

Improve your relationships with your pets

Reduced worry

Enjoy music more

Increased focus

Better relaxation

Increased energy

Enjoy food more

Feeling happier

(3) Name two types of meditation

Multiple choice: select the correct ones:

Sleeping meditation

Mindfulness meditation yoga

Dreaming meditation

Focus on the body

Transcendental meditation

Running meditation

Contemplation meditation

Friendliness meditation

Meditation as taught in this course

(4) What are the benefits of the meditation as taught in this course?

Multiple choice: select the correct ones:

Becoming master of your mind

Becoming calmer

Becoming fitter

Eliminating worry

Lose weight

Relaxation and release of stress

Become a better driver

Removing trauma

Becoming more sensitive

Finding inner stillness

Obtaining self-separation

Stopping smoking

Gaining control of your thoughts

(5) One of the aims of meditation is that we are seeking to control our conscious mind. By doing this, what benefits are we seeking?

Multiple choice: select the correct ones:

Stopping Mechanical worry

Becoming more independent

Stopping anger

Improve our memory

Stopping judging others

Become more intelligent

Removing fear

Stopping feelings of regret

Develop a superior intellect

Stopping negative emotions

(6) It is recommended that Meditation is practiced at least daily for how long?

Multiple choice: select the correct one:

15 Minutes

20 minutes

10 minutes

5 minutes

30 minutes

(7) What are the best times to meditate?

At sunset

In the morning around breakfast time

At a full moon

In the evening after you get home from work

After your evening meal

At sunrise

Now go to the Appendix to check your answers.

Exercise 20 (Section 7):

Introduction to meditation with the IM NA MAH mantra

Go to the Resource Appendix at the end of this journal and access the recording of the Introduction to the IM NA MAH mantra.

Listening to the recording will guide you through the meditation process of using the IM NA MAH mantra, so make yourself comfortable in a place you will not be disturbed for the next 35 minutes and be guided through the meditation listening to my instructions.

How did you get on? You will undoubtedly have experienced many intruding thoughts. This is to be expected when starting to meditate. In the next section I will introduce you to some techniques to help deal with intruding thoughts. However, remember the key technique to use when thoughts intrude, is to gently favour your mantra.

Practice this meditation exercise for at least the next 5 consecutive days once or twice a day.

Record your experiences with the dates here:

Exercise 20 continued:

Exercise 21 (Section 7):
Guided altered state meditation session:

Before you start this exercise, you should have memorised the IM NA MAH mantra in exercise 20 or a suitable mantra of your choice such as Shrim, Hirim or Shiama as I have described in this section. Remember, you should repeat your mantra silently in your mind, not out aloud.

Go to the Resource Appendix at the end of this journal and access the guided altered state meditation audio.

Listen to the guided altered state meditation audio.This is your altered state meditation that should be used once a day every day continuously, preferably twice a day. After you have memorised the instructions on the guided meditation, you can stop using the audio and meditate silently on your own. The choice is yours.

Record you experience here:

Exercise 22 (Section 7):

Workbook journal record for meditation practice section:

Write how you found the meditation in Exercise 21 and keep a record of your experiences below with this technique over the next 30 days. After 30 days it will then become a new habit.

Practice this technique daily. As you practice, I would recommend that you progressively incorporate the techniques taught in the next section, Section 8 Thought and Emotion Control and record your results below with the dates:

Exercise 22 continued:

Exercise 23 (Section 8):

Adding thought rewind and the pause button technique to your daily meditation:

You now need to add this technique of thought control to your regular meditation practice. You don't need to apply it to every intruding thought, but feel free to use it frequently during your meditation. As you practice this technique during every meditation, you will gain a significant degree of control over your thoughts because you will begin to see them as a separate false part of you. Eventually this will expand into your normal daily awareness state of your mind.

Here is a simple summary:

1. During your meditation when you notice you have run off on a train of thoughts, freeze the last one, you can choose to use your imaginary pause button if you wish.
2. See your train of thoughts frozen in front of you just as if you had cut off a length of film and were holding it at arm's length.
3. Now rewind back the imaginary film frame by frame (train of thoughts) linking each thought until you get back to where you departed from your meditation.
4. Continue with your mantra/meditation

Repeat the above steps when appropriate during your meditation. You don't have to do this every time a thought comes into your mind, at other times just gently favour your mantra.

Record your progress below:

Exercise 23 continued:

Exercise 24 (Section 8):
Meditation during adverts

When listening to a commercial radio station focus on only hearing the words. Suspend all mental dialogue. Do not analyse what is being said. Do not judge what is being said. Have no thoughts. Just hear the sound with your internal dialogue suspended and frozen. Just focus on what is being said. Observe only, listen with a silent mind. No opinions or judgments.

Do the same with a visual and audio advert on television for example.

Record your results here with dates over a period of time:

Exercise 24 continued:

Exercise 25 (Section 8):
Meditation In conversations:

When engaged in conversations, observe your reaction to what is being said. What assumption are you making?

On hearing strangers talking in public places. Observe your curiosity, see yourself getting imaginary involved in other people's events. Then stop your thoughts and just hear their words. Listen with silence.

Record your observations on working through this exercise below:

Exercise 26 (Section 8):
Judgments

When thinking about someone, notice your judgments about that person. Observe yourself making that judgment. It is your false self making that judgment. Your higher self does not judge. Record your results below:

Exercise 27 (Section 8)

Meditation when walking

Observe the movement of your legs and arms, keep your head level and observe your surroundings seeing how it changes as you walk. You could pick just one aspect of your surroundings such as the trees, grass, or pavement. Observe only, no internal dialogue, no thinking, no opinions, no judgements.

Record your results below:

Exercise 28 (Section 8): Meditate in idle moments

On the train or bus or in bed for example.

Record your results below:

Exercise 29 (Section 8):

Meditation technique for removing negative feelings & emotions as they arise

Practice this exercise when you feel a negative emotion or thought.

Remember, in this exercise, instead of observing your body as in a progressive relaxation, you are going to be observing your negative feelings and emotions. This can also be done outside of your usual meditation session in a wide-awake state whenever you can stop your daily activity for 5 minutes.

You do this exercise by just silently observing your emotion with absolutely no analytical thoughts. In this way the emotion, the false part of you, will dissolve. The false part dies.

Remember not to think about your emotions when performing this exercise. Observe your feelings and emotions in total mental silence. If a thought comes in, go back to silence each time.

Record your results below:

Exercise 29 continued:

Exercise 30: (Section 8):
Summary of your meditation so far

Write a summary of your daily meditation progress so far:

Exercise 30 continued:

Exercise 31 (Section 9):
Quiz on the Spiritual Part Section:

(1) Whilst practicing self-separation in meditation, which part of you is silently observing your negative emotions or feelings?

(2) What percentage of the mind has consciousness calibration research shown is silent?

(3) Most people think that they are their personality, when in fact they are comprised of so much more! The personality is not eternal, but the higher self is!

Is the above statement True or false?

(4) Which of the following statements can be attributed to Albert Einstein?

    a. "All I want to do is think like God"

    b. "Ultimately, the entire universe has to be understood as a single undivided whole"

    c. "We are slowed down sound and light waves, a walking bundle of frequencies tuned into the cosmos. We are souls dressed up in sacred biochemical garments and our bodies are the instruments through which our souls play their music"

    d. "Thought creates our world, and then says, I didn't do it"

    e. "The more I study science, the more I believe in God"

    f. "I want to know all Gods thoughts; all the rest are just details"

    g. "To change your reality, you have to change your inner thoughts"

(5) What state of meditation gives you access to your higher self, the real you and has a stronger connection to the high spiritual force often referred to as the creator or God?

    a. The transcendental silent state

    b. The conscious state

    c. The dreaming state

    d. The waking state

(6) "Getting in spirit" and going with the flow helps greatly with anxiety and mental health problems. Which of the below are examples of this?

    a. Spending time in nature

    b. Going shopping

    c. Finding a creative hobby or pastime

    d. Gambling

    e. Doing something that really inspires you

    f. Going to lots of parties

    g. Being kind to yourself and others

    h. Always checking your social media

    i. Going with the flow

(7) St Paul said, "That which is seen hath not come from what does appear". What he meant was: matter does not produce matter, it comes from the emptiness, void, and silence. Which of the following statements is true?

    a. This silence is the same as that experienced in the transcendent state of no thoughts in meditation.

    b. You need to enter the transcendent silent state for the full 20 minutes of your meditation to gain benefit.

    c. Only entering the transcendent silent state for a few seconds is very beneficial

    d. Because all matter is created from the silent state this state gives you a stronger connection to the creator and your true self.

e. You need to enter the transcendent silent state for 5 minutes of your meditation to gain benefit.

Now go to the Appendix to check your answers.

Exercise 32 (Section 10):
Quiz on Hypnotherapy and Hypnosis

(1) Assuming you had never been to see a hypnotist or hypnotherapist and you were asked if you'd been hypnotised before, and you replied that you had not. This may be an incorrect answer because:

    a. All hypnosis is self-hypnosis

    b. You can relax easily

    c. In the brief period when you transition from being wide awake to asleep you briefly entered the hypnotic state

    d. When you have been meditating you will most likely have entered at least a light hypnotic state

    e. You can get to sleep quickly

    f. You can remember everything that ever happened to you

    g. When driving your vehicle and subsequently not remembering parts of the journey you would be in a state of hypnosis

    h. You always get a hypnotised feeling

(2) We can determine your brains frequency by hooking it up to a brain frequency EEG monitor of the type found in a hospital. Different frequencies are associated with different levels of consciousness. In which state of consciousness do you experience hypnosis? Is it:

    a. The wide-awake Beta state with a brain frequency of 12 to 38 cycles per second (hertz).

    b. The Alpha state in which we are very relaxed and possibly daydreaming, with a brain frequency of between 8 to 12 cycles per second.

    c. The Theta state in which you will be in a deep meditative state with a brain frequency of 3 to 8 cycles per second.

    d. The Delta state with a brain frequency of 0.5 to 3 cycles per second and is a dreamless state.

(3) Therapy whilst in hypnosis known as hypnotherapy, is predominantly used for two different types of treatments. Select the correct two from the list below:

Cognitive behavioural therapy (CBT)

Analytical therapy

Neurolinguistic programming (NLP)

Suggestion therapy

(4) The earliest references for hypnosis date back to:

Ancient Egypt and Greece

1930

The 17th century

(5) What type of hypnotherapy would be predominantly used for stopping smoking and losing weight?

Analytical therapy

Theta healing

Neurolinguistic programming (NLP)

Suggestion therapy

Group therapy

(6) What type of hypnotherapy would be predominantly used for helping with anxiety, trauma, phobias and emotional and psychological problems?

Analytical therapy

Theta healing

Neurolinguistic programming (NLP)

Suggestion therapy

Group therapy

Now go to the Appendix to check your answers.

Exercise 33:

(Section 10): Self-Hypnosis instruction audio

Go to the Resource Appendix at the end of this journal and access the self-hypnosis instruction audio.

Sit or lie down in a place you will not be disturbed for the next 30 minutes and make yourself comfortable and then listen to the self-hypnosis instruction audio.

Record your experience here:

Exercise 34 (Section 11):
Journal Work
Part 1

Under the following headings write a list of people as it applies to you. Just write what comes to mind. You can take your time and revisit the list many times. So, do not stop because you are having difficulty remembering at any time. You will find more names come each time you go back to writing the list. You may need to continue on additional sheets of paper or pages

Relatives:

Relatives continued:

Friends:

Friends continued:

Partners

Partners

Partners continued:

People you knew at school:

People you knew at school continued:

Work mates

Work mates

Work mates continued:

People related to your hobby or interest:

People related to your hobby or interest continued:

Any significant persons not included above:

Now if applicable, write a list of significant events that you experienced whilst being alone:

Exercise 35 (Section 11):
Journal Work, Part 2

Now write down a list of significant events that occurred whilst you spent time with each person. Do not describe the event in detail, just a limited number of words just sufficient to remind you of that event. Then if applicable, write a list of significant events experienced whilst you were alone.

For now, it is important not to start analysing the event, just observe and list it.

Each list could start in a chronological order if you find that helps. By that I mean from the last or from the first time you met them to the last time of contact, but it is not necessary to do it this way. You will find that each time you go back to working on your list you will remember additional events. Most likely, you will have memories coming back in between writing the list in your journal. So, write them down wherever you are so you can enter them into your journal later.

Exercise 35 Journal work part 2 continued:

Exercise 35 Journal work part 2 continued:

Exercise 35 Journal work part 2 continued:

Exercise 35 Journal work part 2 continued:

Exercise 35 Journal work part 2 continued:

Exercise 36 (Section 11):
Your First Analytical Therapy Session

Conduct a 5-minute review of your memories from your Course Journal.

Set a timer for 1 hour.

Go into self-hypnosis as instructed on the self-hypnosis audio using the audio or memorised procedure.

Go through your memories as instructed in the free association module in this section.

When you feel like ending the session or when you hear the timer sounding at the end of the hour, close the session as described in this section in "Closing the session".

Write a summary of the results in your Course Journal of what you have remembered together with any emotions or feelings experienced. Remember to date your entry. That's it until your next weekly session! If you find memories surfacing in-between sessions which is highly likely, write them down in your Course Journal. Also, write your dreams in your personal Journal if they are notable. You have set up your Personal Journal in Exercise 3.

Exercise 36 continued:

Exercise 37 (Section 11):

Repeat exercise 36, your analytical therapy session regularly:

Write a summary of your experiences during each session, numbering and dating each session. Weekly is ideal.

Session 1 Date:

Session 2   Date:

Session 3   Date:

Exercise 37 continued:

Session 4   Date:

Session 5   Date:

Session 6   Date:

Exercise 37 continued:

Session 7   Date:

Session 8   Date:

Session 9   Date:

Exercise 37 continued:

Session 10   Date:

Session 11   Date:

Session 12   Date:

Exercise 37 continued: Additional Sessions:

Exercise 37 continued: Additional Sessions:

Exercise 38 (Section 12):
End of Course Progression Plan.

Now that you have successfully worked your way through all of the exercises and completed this course, what plans do you have to maintain your continued wellbeing for the future?

What techniques and exercises are you going to continue to use that you have learnt on this course?

What additional new therapies might you consider in the future?

Exercise 39:
Course Evaluation

Are you a member of the Mind Therapy Society? Y/N

Do you feel you benefited from the course greatly, moderately partly or not at all?

Did the course meet your expectations, definitely, mainly, partly or not at all?

To what extent have you acquired new knowledge, developed your skills and changed attitudes as a result of completing this course? Have you learnt very little, learned a satisfactory amount or learnt a considerable amount?

Was the course organised and taught in a satisfactory way?
Yes/No/ comments:

Were the teaching materials used satisfactory? Yes/No/comments:

If you were subscribing to paid support, was the feedback and support with your progress satisfactory? (Yes/No/comments)

How would you briefly summarise your experience of the course?

Would you recommend the course to anyone else?

Any other comments?

APPENDIX 1:
Answers to Quizzes'

Exercise 19 (Section 6):
Quiz: Introduction to Meditation

(1) What are the two stages of meditation?

Answer: Mindfulness and thoughtless awareness

(2) Name 5 observed benefits of meditation
All correct answers:

Help with mental health problems

Lower blood pressure

Reduced stress levels

Help with sleep

Help with Post-traumatic stress disorder

Help with Addictions

Reduced Worry

Increased focus

Better relaxation

Increased energy

Feeling happier

(3) Name two types of meditation

All correct answers:

Focus on the body

Mindfulness meditation yoga

Contemplation meditation

Transcendental meditation

Meditation as taught in this course

(4) What are the benefits of the meditation as taught in this course?

All correct answers:

Becoming master of your mind

Becoming calmer

Eliminating worry

Relaxation and release of stress

Removing trauma

Finding inner stillness

Obtaining self-separation

Gaining control of your thoughts

(5) One of the aims of meditation is that we are seeking to control our conscious mind. By doing this, what benefits are we seeking?

All correct answers:

Stopping Mechanical worry

Stopping anger

Stopping judging others

Removing fear

Stopping feelings of regret

Stopping negative emotions

(6) It is recommended that Meditation is practiced at least daily for how long?

Answer: 20 minutes

(7) What are the best times to meditate?

Answer:

In the morning around breakfast time

In the evening after you get home from work

After your evening meal

Exercise 31 (Section 9):

Quiz on the Spiritual Part Section:

(1) Whilst practicing self-separation in meditation, which part of you is silently observing your negative emotions or feelings?

Answer: Your higher self, spiritual self or soul.

(2) What percentage of your mind has consciousness calibration research shown is silent?

Answer: 99%

(3) Most people think that they are their personality, when in fact they are comprised of so much more! The personality is not eternal, but the higher self is!

Is the above statement True or false?

Answer: True

(4) Which of the following statements can be attributed to Albert Einstein?

Answers:

All I want to do is think like God"

"We are slowed down sound and light waves, a walking bundle of frequencies tuned into the cosmos. We are souls dressed up in sacred biochemical garments and our bodies are the instruments through which our souls play their music"

"The more I study science, the more I believe in God"

"I want to know all Gods thoughts; all the rest are just details"

The other quotes are from David Bohm

(5) What state of meditation gives you access to your higher self, the real you and has a stronger connection to the high spiritual force often referred to as the creator or God?

Answer:

The Transcendental Silent State

(6) "Getting in spirit" and going with the flow helps greatly with anxiety and mental health problems. Which of the below are examples of this?

Answers:

Spending time in nature

Finding a creative hobby or pastime

Do something that really inspires you

Being kind to yourself and others

Going with the flow

(7) St Paul said, "That which is seen hath not come from what does appear". What he meant was: matter does not produce matter, it comes from the emptiness, void, and silence. Which of the following statements is true?

Answers:

This silence is the same as that experienced in the transcendent state of no thoughts in meditation.

Only entering the transcendent silent state for a few seconds is very beneficial.

Because all matter is created from the silent state this state gives you a stronger connection to the creator and your true self.

Exercise 32 (Section 10):

Quiz on Hypnotherapy and Hypnosis

If you were asked if you'd been hypnotised before, and you replied that you had not. This may be an incorrect answer because:

Answers:

All hypnosis is self-hypnosis

In the brief period when you transition from being wide awake to asleep you briefly entered the hypnotic state

When you have been meditating you will most likely have entered at least a light hypnotic state

When driving your vehicle and subsequently not remembering the journey, you would be in a state of hypnosis

(2) We can determine your brains frequency by hooking it up to an EEG monitor of the type found in a hospital. Different frequencies are associated with different levels of consciousness. In which state of consciousness do you experience hypnosis?

Answer:

The Alpha state of consciousness

(3) Therapy whilst in hypnosis known as hypnotherapy, is predominantly used for two different types of treatments. Select the correct two from the list below:

Answer:

Analytical therapy

Suggestion therapy

(4) The earliest references for hypnosis date back to:

Answer: Ancient Egypt and Greece

(5) What type of hypnotherapy would be predominantly used for stopping smoking and losing weight?

Answer: Suggestion therapy

(6) What type of hypnotherapy would be predominantly used for helping with anxiety, trauma, phobias and emotional and psychological problems?

Answer: Analytical therapy

APPENDIX 2:
Resources & Support

AUDIO SUPPORT DOWNLOADS

(Information correct on 9 March 2023)

Go to the authors web site for this course to listen to the audio guides below at: **www.anxietytherapy.info**

Downloads available for:

Exercise 4: Guided meditation/relaxation/hypnotherapy audio.

Exercise 20: Introduction to the IM NA MAH mantra

Exercise 21: Guided altered state meditation audio
Exercise 33: Self-hypnosis instruction audio

To download a copy of the Course Journal for your personal use go to: **www.anxietytherapy.info**

FREE NEWSLETTER

You can subscribe to The Mind Therapy Society Newsletter for help and Advice at **www.anxietytherapy.info**

For more information, help and support visit: **www.mindtherapysociety.com**

The author (Paul Craddock) contact details:

Email: paul@healthyandwise.co.uk

Books website: www.healthyandwise.co.uk

Therapy website: www.mindtherapyclinic.org

[i] Neil French, Successful Hypnotherapy
[ii] Sigmund Freud 1. Introductory Lectures on Psychoanalysis Lecture 24, The Common Neurotic State
[iii] Dr C. G. Jung

Printed in Great Britain
by Amazon

20374414R00106